F

I DAR

MW00779551

"Sylvia draws from her own suc
to guide the reader through a variety of strateg...
emotional intelligence relatable in a way that puts it immediately within our
reach. She helps us remove our fears about confronting our emotions. Her
lucid writing explores the behaviors critical to honest self-examination and to
surmounting self-imposed obstacles."

~ **MARK ALLAN WILLIAMS,** 30+ year Editor at Bloomberg,
Journalist, and Essayist

"In *I Dare You to Care*, Sylvia artfully uses personal and professional storytelling
to transform what could be a complex topic into something we can all really
understand and apply with greater ease."

~ **GARLAND NIXON,** Political Commentator,
Pacifica Network and Fox News

"A must-read for students and young professionals everywhere. In a world where
you will compete with others of equal or greater skill than you, your emotional
intelligence and the strategies Sylvia shares in this book will set you head and
shoulders above the crowd."

~ **DR. BERNARD DEMCZUK,** Historian, former Assistant VP at George
Washington University

"Sylvia has a gift for communicating an intellectual topic with a captivating
conversational tone. Through her inspirational message, she effectively
instructs and assists the reader along a step-by-step path to improved emotional
intelligence."

~ **MARIE HUNT,** Veteran Educator, New York State School System

"Emotional Intelligence is universal in its depth and breadth, but intensely
individual as well. What I loved about editing this book was that the topic
resonates with every audience. The corporate CEO will learn as much from the
lessons within this book as the recent college grad or the stay-at-home mom or
the blossoming entrepreneur."

~ **KRISTIN CLARK TAYLOR,** Author, Journalist, and former White House
Communications Strategist

Thank you for joining me
on this journey. May these
pages be a meaningful
companion as you navigate
your life's streets with
greater emotional intelligence!

My Best Wishes,
Sylvia Baffour

I DARE YOU TO CARE

Using Emotional Intelligence to Inspire,
Influence, and Achieve Remarkable Growth

SYLVIA BAFFOUR

www.amplifypublishing.com

I Dare You To Care

Cover design by Joanna Kosmides Edwards

Second Printing. This Amplify Publishing edition printed in 2024

For more information, please contact:
Mascot Books
620 Herndon Parkway, Suite 320
Herndon, VA 20170
info@mascotbooks.com

Library of Congress Control Number: 2019900366

CPSIA Code: PRV0624B
ISBN-13: 978-1-64307-258-6

Printed in the United States

I dedicate this book to my irreplaceable parents, Eric and Emma Baffour. Still the kindest, most generous, and thoughtful human beings I've known.

CONTENTS

INTRODUCTION 1

SECTION ONE

THE ESSENCE OF EMOTIONAL INTELLIGENCE (EI) 6

CHAPTER 1 What It Is and What It Isn't 7
The foundational components of emotional intelligence

CHAPTER 2 Self-Awareness and Self-Mastery. 19
A look at how our emotions help us or harm us

CHAPTER 3 Empathy and Relationship Management 36
Connect effectively with others and build your influence and impact

SECTION TWO

WHY CARE? 51

CHAPTER 4 Your Personal Growth Depends on It 52
How EI makes you really enjoyable to be around

CHAPTER 5 Your Professional Growth Depends on It 65
How EI increases your effectiveness in the workplace

CHAPTER 6 Your Effect on Others Matters 81
How we consciously and unconsciously impact others around us

SECTION THREE

DARING TO CARE HAS ITS REWARDS 95

CHAPTER 7 Identifying and Maximizing the Emotional Benefits   96
Manage your emotions, stress, and uncertainty like a pro

CHAPTER 8 Touching (and Embracing) the Tangible Rewards . 110
Handle change, conflict, and leadership challenges like a pro

CHAPTER 9 The Courage that Comes from Clarity 126
Embrace life's discomforts and difficulties with greater ease

CHAPTER 10 Let the Journey Begin! 140
Ten emotionally intelligent habits worth remembering

CONCLUSION

My Final, Five-Word Challenge 157

ACKNOWLEDGMENTS 163

ABOUT THE AUTHOR 166

INTRODUCTION

I COULDN'T BELIEVE MY CLOSEST friend, Mavis, didn't warn me. Just a day earlier, we'd spent a lot of time together on the campus of our all-girls public school in Zimbabwe. Throughout the past two years at our school, Mavis and I bonded over the fact that we were the only two to leave our homes and loved ones for a foreign land. With our families being so distant, we were like family to each other.

Little did I know that I would soon come face-to-face with twelve angry 15-year-olds, primed and ready to give me a piece of their minds. That evening, my dormmates all sat huddled around a few beds. Some were sitting on wooden footlockers. I walked into the ravenous glare of their hungry eyes, waiting for the green light from our Dorm Prefect who motioned me in to sit down and hear the girls out.

My heart summersaulted from my chest into my mouth. What could I possibly have done wrong? These girls were all clearly here because of me. To my surprise, Mavis sat squarely in the middle of all of them.

And then the verbal assault began. So much was said, but these final words stung the most: "Sylvia, you are a know-it-all," and, "You make everyone feel worthless and small around you," and even, "You're very arrogant and full of yourself."

My 15-year-old heart was crushed. Tears streamed down my face in pain and disbelief. How in the world could I be *any* of these horrible things that they accused me of? I thought they were my friends. Especially Mavis. As my tears dried up, anger and resentment flooded in. I was determined not to speak to any of them again. I didn't need them anyway.

Or so I thought.

Despite having to see my dormmates every day since that horrible confrontation, I kept my promise. I didn't speak to any of them and they didn't speak to me. After a couple of weeks of self-imposed silence, my bitterness began to fade.

It was then that I noticed thoughts flooding in that had me questioning whether they could have been right. *Had some of their earlier, cruel comments actually been accurate? Could some of their stinging observations actually have been on target?*

All along I felt betrayed and persecuted. I believed that *they* were wrong. But being by myself during those two weeks of self-imposed isolation had given me time to think and reflect. It was during one of these moments of deep reflection when I had a "light-bulb" moment; a moment of shining clarity and clear-sighted reflection.

All those times I thought I was entertaining and expanding their minds, through my adventures having lived in several countries, I had instead been making them feel "less-than" for only having lived in one country. I didn't intend to make them feel the way they said I did. In reality, what ought to have mattered was that they experienced me very differently from my intentions. In other words, I needed to put myself in their shoes a heck of a lot more empathetically than I did. But I was simply incapable.

With this newfound wisdom, I made a commitment to get as far away as possible from being the kind of person who made others feel uncomfortable and small. I vowed to become more aware of how others were feeling around me.

It was this very quest to reinvent myself—this initial desire to heighten my own awareness of how I actually made other people feel—which led to my interest in emotional intelligence, even when I didn't know what to call it.

This is the spark that lit the flame.

How aware we are of our emotions and how effective we are at managing their impact on our relationships is the essence of what is commonly referred to as Emotional Intelligence (EI). And it is this emotional intelligence that helps us better deal with uncertainty and change, build empathy, reduce conflict, and strengthen our personal and professional relationships.

The journey towards EI is continuous; it is not a destination. It's a journey that requires discipline, awareness, and daily practice. I've devoted the past 18 years to this journey, as a Certified Life Coach, mentor and professional speaker, and to guiding individuals and organizations towards achieving radical results with emotionally intelligent strategies.

My journey towards EI has become my way of life, on both a personal and professional level—and my desire now is to share all that I have learned. This is why I'm writing this book.

While emotional intelligence continues to gain in popularity as a necessary skillset for personal and professional growth, many people struggle with bridging the gap. The gap between understanding its immense value and actually doing the hard work to become more emotionally intelligent can often be wide and yawning. But when you invest time and personal focus on doing the work, the result is a better and more successful *you.*

What I want to do in writing this book is to help you become better able to identify and manage your emotions; raise your awareness of how others feel, and improve and deepen your relationships in order to become more effective in all walks of your life.

I Dare You to Care is an invitation to join me on this journey—to discover the power of emotional intelligence and witness its transformative impact on your daily life.

Join me as we explore the answers to these questions:

- How can I use my emotions to work for me and not against me?
- Why should I give a *#@* about how others feel?
- What does it take to have more satisfying and rewarding relationships?

We'll explore these powerful questions. We'll delve into the possible answers. Most important, we'll use this book as a roadmap to guide us along on our EI journey and to chart a course towards a heightened state of emotional awareness. This is EI at its very, very best, and our journey could be life-changing.

So come along for the ride.

SECTION ONE

THE ESSENCE
OF EMOTIONAL
INTELLIGENCE (EI)

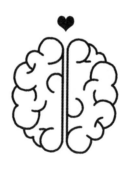

CHAPTER 1
What It Is and What It Isn't

*"We are dangerous when we are not conscious of our
responsibility for how we behave, think, and feel."*
– Marshall B. Rosenberg

NOTHING FELT UNUSUAL ABOUT MY final week waiting tables at B. Smith's restaurant in Washington, D.C. on January 17, 2001. That was, until I spotted one of the most renowned and influential voices of our time. A beloved American icon, sitting at the cigar bar, enjoying a Martini and our signature red beans and rice. I begged my friend Candace, who was bartending, to introduce me to her. All I wanted was to say hello and get back to work.

Completely star-struck, I walked up to her, hands trembling, knees knocking. "Dr. Angelou! I just wanted to say hello and tell you how much I enjoy your work!"

She nodded graciously before replying in her regal, resonant voice, "Very nice to meet you, young lady."

As I turned around to walk back to my section, she tapped me on the shoulder and began asking me questions about who I was and what I wanted to do next in life. We had countless celebrities dine at B. Smith's over the years and most wouldn't give you the time of day, beyond a quick nod or smile.

I had just co-authored a soon-to-be-published book and was looking forward to starting my own Life Coaching practice. The distinguished Dr. Angelou asked me if I had a business card, and I said yes. I always kept them inside my apron, which I had taken off and left in the kitchen. The next words she uttered sent me racing to the back of the kitchen.

"Go and get your business card and give it to me. I'm going to give it to someone—and if they call you, it may be the best thing that ever happened to you," she said with her characteristic poise and power.

As if that wasn't enough, she later invited me to join her and her family for their annual Thanksgiving Day celebration at her home in Winston-Salem, N.C.

A year after our first encounter, I called her travel companion, Lydia Stuckey, to see if I could speak to her for a few minutes about a career dilemma. Instead of a phone conversation, Dr. Angelou instructed Ms. Stuckey to invite me to visit her in her comfortable brownstone in Harlem the following week.

On the bus ride to New York City, I couldn't contain my competing feelings of intense nervousness and child-like excitement. I could hardly believe that I was about to spend alone time with Dr. Maya Angelou. Thoughts flooded my mind that had me questioning how I got so lucky. What in the world would I say to her? I hoped I wouldn't make a fool of myself by saying the wrong thing!

I walked into her beautiful basement kitchen in Harlem. Bright, sun-kissed walls radiated with warmth, filling her place with an inviting Southern charm. It wasn't until my first hour into chatting with Dr. Angelou in her kitchen that I understood who she had wanted to connect me with a year earlier: It was David Lacamera, her booking agent.

While I sat across from her, she called him on the phone and asked him to help me as much as he could with my professional speaking journey. I was humbled beyond belief, and deeply grateful.

"*Why me?*" I thought, as I watched the regal woman hang up the phone. My heart skipped a beat and the butterflies in my belly took full flight.

On the five-hour bus ride home to Washington, D.C., after two unforgettable hours with her, I reflected on something she told me that has stuck with me to this day. I'd asked her why she'd gone to the trouble of connecting me with her booking agent— someone who obviously booked only high-value or celebrity speakers, when I was neither.

"Ms. Baffour," she answered with her characteristic grace, "I have come a long way and overcome a lot in my life. I don't take my blessings for granted or those who believed in me more than I believed in myself in those early days. These, Ms. Baffour (she never called me by my first name), are *your* early days. Just stay focused and keep striving."

Dr. Angelou had no idea just how much of a flame she lit inside me that day. Her words of wisdom and encouragement sparked a fire within me. I was determined to succeed and I was determined to make her proud.

To me, Dr. Maya Angelou was a walking example of Emotional Intelligence (EI) at its best, and fortunately for me, I was able to personally witness this constant display of EI during the remaining twelve years I interacted with her. In a very real way, she helped *define* Emotional Intelligence; she taught me more about this powerful paradigm than perhaps any other individual: She was the teacher, and I was the student.

What I was privileged and humbled to experience firsthand were some of the very principles she left behind for us all, particularly these wise words that she is now most remembered by: "*I've learned that people will forget what you said, people will forget what you did, but people will never forget how you made them feel.*"

While the central focus of EI is about how effectively we manage the impact of our emotions on others, one of the stand-out qualities of emotionally intelligent people is their ability to see the best in others. As an accomplished and globally recognized poet and civil rights activist, Maya Angelou refused to let her celebrity status get in the way of making time for others, and making others feel valued.

No matter who you were, when you were around her, she made you feel like you were the most important person in the room. Her ability to empathize with others was absolutely remarkable.

There is, indeed, a lot for us to review and examine on our journey towards a deeper understanding of EI, and much to grasp as we try to more fully understand its benefits and applicability in our own daily lives. Before we move much further, though, I feel obliged to dispel a few myths floating around. Once we get a sense of what EI is *not*, we can move right on to exploring more of what it *is*.

Myth #1: EI IS SOMETHING YOU ARE BORN WITH

Being "born with something"—especially if it is a positive trait— often conjures up the incorrect assumption that this trait (whatever it is) is something you didn't have to work to obtain.

If, for instance, you happen to be a "Brainiac" with a genius IQ over 160, the assumption is that you ace exams and tests without studying for them. Similarly, if you were born with considerable athletic talent, then the assumption, perhaps, is that you don't have to work as hard as everyone else to make it to the top of your sporting platform.

The reality is that even those born with unmatched talent have to work to hone their natural abilities. Harnessing the power of emotional intelligence is no different.

While it is true that some people might have an innate ability to connect with their emotions and the emotions of others, it is still something they have to work on. The good news is that EI is something that *can* be learned by most of us. Put simply: Emotional Intelligence can be acquired, learned and honed over time; it is not necessarily or exclusively innate.

And here, I share what I will call an "essential truth" about EI; a directive, of sorts, that will help you own your journey: Learn how to better recognize and understand your own emotions, manage how they affect you at any given moment and understand how to better connect with what others are feeling.

The naked truth about EI is that it is a skillset that *does* require constant work, but one nevertheless that comes with immeasurable rewards. And the good news—again—is that it can be acquired, honed and measured over time.

Myth #2: HIGH SELF-AWARENESS = HIGH EMOTIONAL INTELLIGENCE

Having a strong grasp on your own emotions, i.e., a heightened sense of self-awareness, is certainly an important foundation upon which emotional intelligence is built. But self-awareness alone is not enough. That is why it's a mistake to assume that high self-awareness is synonymous with high emotional intelligence. *It is not.*

Let's try to break down this myth by using this example: If you have a driver's license and the keys to a car, what good are they to you if you never get in to drive to your desired destination? Put simply, what good is *having* the tools if you don't *use* them?

You can be very aware of and in tune with your own emotions at any given moment, but if you do nothing to *manage* these emotions, particularly in difficult and challenging situations, you are at a distinct disadvantage. In other words, being self-aware is of little use if you cannot also focus upon self-*management.* The good and bad news here is that managing your emotions is a choice. (And as I mentioned in Myth #1, it is often an acquired skill.)

Perhaps you've heard the saying, "It's not what happens to you, but how you *react* to what happens to you that counts." Anything that challenges or triggers us is bound to stir up some sort of emotion within us. While we may not be able to control our circumstance, we have the power to control what we do with our emotions.

I believe that the emotions we feel are physiological and much less influenced by us. Sometimes you can't help that initial feeling of anger or sadness that hits you. However, what you choose to do in those moments that you feel what you feel, is fully in your control and ultimately what matters most.

When it comes to showing high levels of EI, you have to go beyond simply being aware of your own emotions. You have to propel yourself towards a more heightened state of mind where you are able to control what you do with how you feel.

At the 2018 U.S. Open Women's Tennis final, Serena Williams' bid for a 24th Grand Slam title came to a crashing end with three unprecedented code-of-conduct violations handed to her by the chair umpire, Carlos Ramos.

She was first accused of illegally receiving coaching from her coach, Patrick Mouratoglou, and was given a warning for that violation. Because she believed she hadn't received any on-court coaching, this accusation incensed her and began her emotional downward spiral.

As the game went on, she received a penalty for breaking her racket after losing a crucial point. This cost her a point in the next game, when her Japanese opponent, Naomi Osaka, was serving.

Her third violation was for verbal abuse of an official. This resulted in her forfeiting an entire game, which sent her into an even deeper emotional tailspin. Sadly, she never recovered from this and lost the match in straight sets, depriving the viewing public of the full enjoyment of what promised to be a great match between two heavy-hitting rivals.

While most who watched the match agree that the chair umpire could have done more to de-escalate the situation, Serena had a role to play as well. Her inability to manage what she did with how she felt on the court cost her a chance at making history by equaling the all-time Grand Slam record currently held by Margaret Court of Australia.

While Serena's story may sound extreme, it is one that many of us can relate to, to some extent. Can you think back to a particularly trying or challenging situation in your life? Did your emotions take over and get the best of you?

Your ability to become more self-aware and self-managed influences the actions you take in any situation. This, in turn, can impact those around you, for better or worse. In the next chapter, we'll explore self-awareness and self-mastery more deeply, in an effort to understand how we can tap into the essential tools that will help us raise our levels.

Myth #3: EMPATHY IS ABOUT "BEING NICE"

Empathy has nothing to do with trying to please people, agreeing with them, or telling them exactly what they want to hear. Neither is it dependent on how much of a people-pleaser you are. Being empathic requires you to be present and engaged in how someone else is feeling, simple as that. It should not be mistaken with merely *being nice*.

The idea of "being nice," in this case, implies that your goal is simply to do everything you can to get along with others, regardless of whether you truly empathize with someone else's emotions or not. This does a disservice to everyone involved. Why? Because usually this notion of "being nice" is often employed simply to soothe our own ego and make us look good in the eyes of others. Sure, expressing kindness and compassion is essential, but it is always important to check your motive; to assess where that "need for niceness" is really originating.

The fact is, you can disagree with someone and still show empathy. Practicing empathy doesn't mean that you lose your ground in stepping over to where someone else stands. While being nice is certainly a healthy ingredient that helps us show empathy, it is not the defining component of empathy itself.

If, for instance, you are a leader, you might have to be stern and therefore "not very nice" to get an important point across or take a decisive and/or unpopular action—yet you can still show empathy while doing it!

As part of my research for this book, I interviewed numerous business leaders to find out about their experiences with emotional intelligence in the workplace.

One particular leader's story stuck in my mind because of the gut-wrenching decision he had to make in laying off fifteen percent of his staff. These were folks who had been with the company for a long time, and he had gotten to know most of them personally. The directive to lay them off came from the company's board and shareholders and he felt helpless at his inability to save their jobs.

Each staff member who was notified that they were to be laid off got called into his office, individually. He took time to listen to them and acknowledge their feelings and fears. He then offered to help each of them find new employment and give them a personal recommendation.

This was clearly a compassionate touch rarely afforded to most people laid off from their jobs. While the decision he had to make was "not nice," he understood the need for empathy and he committed to doing what he could to make the most out of a very difficult situation.

Myth #4: A HIGH EI SHIELDS YOU FROM DIFFICULT EMOTIONS

As many psychologists have suggested, there are six basic emotions that are universal throughout and across human cultures: Fear, disgust, anger, surprise, happiness and sadness. Countless other emotions we feel are, for the most part, a variation of one of the six identified above.

Let's take a closer look: Excitement, for instance, is often a variation of happiness, and contempt, a variation of anger. These basic emotions, scaled up or down, produce many of the other emotions we feel at any given moment.

It's possible that at times, we inadvertently mix up the difference between our emotions and our mood. What's the difference?

It is widely believed that emotions tend to be short-lived but intense, and they are likely to have a definite and identifiable cause. A mood, on the other hand, tends to be milder than an emotion, but longer lasting.

Consider this scenario that illustrates the difference: Your boss walks into your office at 5:30 p.m. on a Friday, as you are getting ready to walk out the door for a fun-filled weekend. He drops a big file of papers—an unexpected project—on your desk and tells you he expects you to have it completed by 9:00 a.m. on Monday morning.

I venture to say that you will probably feel some anger at the fact that he waited until the last minute, thus putting you in a position of having to spend your weekend working. Gone are your dreams of a fun-filled weekend!

The initial *emotion* of anger that you feel might not be long-lasting, but the *mood* it triggers could leave you feeling resentful and frustrated for the entire weekend and beyond.

In this case, your sour mood can be linked directly back to what happened when your boss walked in, snatching you away from the joyous prospect of a much-anticipated weekend of family fun and frolic.

At times, a steady accumulation of annoyances throughout the day might be responsible for our mood—or a variety of other unexpected circumstances that we can't always put our finger upon. Because our moods can sustain themselves far beyond the offending incident, they can often morph into *other* kinds of moods that make identifying the root cause even more challenging. Put simply, moods and emotions can often get muddled in the mix.

As human beings, we don't get to move through our lives without experiencing an array of emotions. There isn't a soul on this planet who can stand up and honestly profess that they've only experienced positive emotions.

The reality is that emotions are natural, instinctive and visceral. Having high EI doesn't shield you from feeling frustration, anger, resentment and other negative emotions. What it *does* do, though, is guide you towards being more self-regulated in ways that prevent you from acting out on your difficult emotions. Unlike robots, we have the ability to feel, and thankfully, we also have the ability to control what we do about how we feel.

People with a high EI feel difficult emotions as deeply and as viscerally as anyone else. The essential difference, however, is that these people spend time building up their self-awareness and ability to regulate their emotions in a way that guides their behavior in positive and productive directions. They become keenly aware of how they feel when they are negatively triggered, and they rely on coping tools and techniques to help them manage those reactions.

To summarize this chapter, let's delve again into the very essence of EI, deep into its definition: *Emotional Intelligence is the ability to identify different emotions, understand their effect on you and others, and use that information to guide your thinking and behavior.*

The journey to growing one's emotional intelligence is a road less travelled. It requires constant work on ourselves, and that takes courage. It's not easy to peel back your ego to self-reflect and self-manage. It's not easy to step into someone else's shoes, however uncomfortable.

As Dr. Angelou reminded me constantly, this is work worth doing. This is important, challenging work, and I consider myself fortunate to have learned, first-hand, from a woman, a visionary, of her stoicism and stature.

No, she and I are no longer sitting together in her sun-splashed kitchen in New York. But the lessons she taught me back then (and in the years that came after) are lessons that will last a lifetime.

It is these lessons—and countless others I've learned along my life's journey—that I want to share with you now.

CHAPTER 2
Self-Awareness and Self-Mastery

"When awareness is brought to an emotion, power is brought to your life."
– Tara Meyer Robson

IN THE FALL OF 1999, I believed I had the perfect job as a business consultant with one of the top global accounting and consulting firms. I was set to transfer from the Washington, D.C., office to the Toronto, Canada office. My U.S. work visa was expiring and I had a better chance of getting a permanent work visa if I moved to Canada.

With excitement and eager anticipation, I ended my apartment lease in Annandale, Virginia. I had a farewell party. I even picked out a lovely apartment in a high-rise building overlooking magnificent Lake Ontario.

This new arrangement would have me flying to Washington, D.C. during the week for work and then enjoying a sinfully good time on the weekends in the lively city of Toronto. At the ripe old age of twenty-two, I couldn't have imagined a better life.

Two weeks before my departure, I found myself in the office of a senior partner at the firm. I couldn't understand why his face was beet red, but I knew it wasn't good.

"Sylvia," he said with a trembling voice, "I am so very sorry to be the one to have to tell you this."

I held my breath, not quite sure of what was to come. He continued:

"We can no longer send you to the Toronto office and the Washington, D.C. office cannot sponsor your work visa, either. We didn't realize that having you work here while living in Canada would require you to have a work permit in both countries. Filing for both permits permanently cancelled out your current work status."

I couldn't believe my ears. I was absolutely shattered and heartbroken. I had recently won the firm's "Unsung Hero" award, rare and prestigious recognition from the firm that had never been previously earned by anyone at my consultant level. I had worked so hard over the past year to prove myself to be an asset to the firm. Surely there was something they could do to help me?

It was not to be.

So here I was, with fifteen days before I had to uproot myself and my life from the United States.

I had lost my apartment, my income, my dream job. As I slumped in the chair listening to the partner deliver this horrible news, feelings of disappointment, hopelessness and rage were brewing inside me. This felt like a betrayal. They weren't even *fighting* for me!

Suddenly, shockingly, my manic mind was interrupted by the invasion of a single thought: A powerful piece of advice I'd once heard from renowned spiritual teacher Gary Zukav, on *Oprah*.

Mr. Zukav, famous for his enlightenment and wisdom, said, "You must never use *negative emotions* to make an important decision in your life and expect to have a positive outcome."

Well, I sure as heck was facing a vitally important life decision and I knew for sure that I was feeling a tremendous amount of anger and fear, wondering how my life's path had taken such a dramatic downturn.

For me, Mr. Zukav's words were grounding. They anchored me to something larger than my own anxiety. This, for me, was a powerful, pivotal moment in that it helped me identify my emotions and decide how to harness them in a productive way.

Holding onto those difficult emotions, as dejected as I felt, and as legitimate and well-justified as they were, prevented me from reacting to the situation in a way that was unproductive. I didn't want my emotions to control me to the point that I might do (or say) something I might later regret. While I believe I had every right to be angry and frustrated, I didn't want my emotions ruling me and thereby dictating my response to this overwhelming situation.

Mr. Zukav's words of wisdom gave me a little head space to pause; a little extra space to dig deep and think about what else I could do to stay in the United States legally. Slowly but surely, through the fog and the haze, a clear-sighted solution emerged: Graduate school!

Jumping into graduate school became my saving grace and it bought me an additional eighteen months in the country.

Reflecting on this experience brought an inescapable truth to light. The way *we feel* in one moment, directly impacts what *we do* in the next. The more we understand our own emotions, the better positioned we are to use them in a way that helps us rather than harms us.

This is why self-awareness is such a foundational step in the journey to becoming more emotionally intelligent. We cannot begin to master our emotions if we don't first understand them and their effect on us.

Before we examine some ways to enhance our self-awareness and our ability to master our emotions, let's dig deeper into a fuller understanding of our emotions.

What We Need to Know about Emotions

Emotions are a vital part of life; they communicate a lot about us in any given moment. Our emotions are essentially segmented into three components:

- How we experience them;
- How our bodies react to them; and,
- How we behave in response to what we feel.

While many tend to categorize emotions as either negative or positive, it's rather how we perceive our emotions that make them so. If you think about it, even emotions that we associate with being negative—like fear—can be useful to us (and in some cases, even life-saving, if we use our fight-or-flight fear response as an example).

If, for instance, you find yourself in a situation that intuitively feels dangerous, the fear you feel can become a great teacher and a powerful motivator to guide you towards safety, escape or relief. Ultimately, it is our reaction to our emotions and not the actual *feeling* that they create that carries the potential for a negative outcome.

At the end of the day, as I've already mentioned, emotions are part of our human experience, so we can't just command them to magically disappear with the simple snap of a finger. Instead of focusing our energy on trying not to feel what we're feeling, we're far better off if we can use that same energy to manage what *we do* with how *we feel*.

It's important for us to also realize that *we are not our emotions*. The moment we define ourselves by our emotions, they have control over us. If you *are* your emotions, then you make it difficult to separate yourself—and thus, your actions—from them, and this renders you essentially powerless and dangerously vulnerable.

If, for instance, your colleague fails to submit their portion of an important document you urgently need to give to a client, I'm sure this is something that would probably anger and frustrate you.

While you have every right to feel these feelings, it is important that you remain mindful of the words you use to describe your emotions. If you say, "I *am* so angry at John for dropping the ball on this critical assignment," without realizing it, you've become that emotion in a way that binds you to it.

If you instead say, "I *feel* really angry that John dropped the ball…" you are still acknowledging how you feel, but you are separating how you feel from who you are, and from what you are going to do as a result of those feelings. By saying, "I *feel* angry," rather than, "I *am* angry," you used deliberate language to convey your state of feeling and not your state of being.

Do you see the difference? The former allows you to more quickly let go of the emotion and focus your energy on what you can do about it.

When it comes to emotions, it's critical to remember that you always have the power of choice. You can choose, at any given moment, how you will react to the things you experience in life. Just because you don't have control over what you instinctively feel doesn't mean that you cannot control what happens within you.

Your ability to choose how you react, even in the most overwhelming of situations or circumstances, is what earns you the reputation of being someone who is very self-aware and self-managed—and therefore very measured, thoughtful and emotionally intelligent.

As we look at the following three scenarios, I invite you to consider how you would feel and react in each instance. Jot down your thoughts on the empty lines so that you can reflect on them later:

Scenario A

You order a shirt online that you really want to wear to your much-anticipated high school reunion. The shirt arrives in two days, as promised. With excitement and anticipation, you open up the box, hold up the shirt and immediately realize something is wrong. Darn it! The company sent you the wrong shirt ... and your reunion is tomorrow night! It's past the company's office hours, so you can't speak with anyone until tomorrow morning, and what's worse: You don't have anything else to wear!

What are the immediate emotions you feel?

_____

_____

_____

What would you do about how you feel?

_____

_____

_____

If you feel some measure of frustration, as is probably the case, then you had a similar reaction to my friend Dave. Here's what happened to him recently: In spite of feeling frustrated and annoyed at the company's mistake, he decided against impulsively sending an angry e-mail to them, giving them an earful about what he thought of their carelessness and unprofessionalism.

Instead, he took a few minutes to think about what he would say in his e-mail: How would he behave as a result of what had happened? Would he be able to direct his actions in a way that differentiates them from his emotions? Well, he did just that!

In a measured and very civil e-mail, Dave was able to politely tell them that they shipped the wrong shirt. He also told them that since there was no time to get his hands on the correct shirt, he would just wear the one they sent and not worry about it.

To his surprise (and delight), he received an e-mail reply from the company *that same night,* apologizing for their mistake. In addition to confirming that he could keep the shirt that they mistakenly delivered, they shipped the correct one overnight—and it arrived in time for his reunion. They'd even enclosed a nice card: "Thanks for being awesome. Many people would've handled that in a much different, less kind way."

Jot down here the lessons you learned about emotional intelligence from this scenario. How will you apply these lessons to your own EI development?

_____

_____

_____

Scenario B

Imagine you're a world-class athlete, preparing to swim the race of your life. You're poised on the starting block, waiting for the sound of the gun. *Bang!* You dive headlong into the water—but something immediately goes wrong with your goggles. They malfunction and begin to fill with water, which severely impedes your vision and slows your speed considerably.

What are the immediate emotions you feel?

_____

_____

_____

What would you do about how you feel?

_____

_____

_____

This very same scenario happened to the most decorated U.S. Olympic swimmer, Michael Phelps, during the 2008 Beijing Olympic Games. The water in his goggles got so bad that he couldn't even see the wall when he touched it with his final stroke. Instead of panicking, he remained calm. His sole focus—his primary and *only* goal—was to win the race.

Not only did he go on to win the race, he set a world record and went on to win the first of eight gold medals at those Olympic Games. It's fair to say that most people would have gotten frustrated, panicked and lost momentum.

Reflect on Phelps' mastery of emotions in this challenging situation. How would you adapt similarly in a difficult situation?

_____

_____

_____

Scenario C

You get a phone call asking you to get on the first flight possible to be with an ailing loved one whose health has taken a sudden turn for the worse. It'll take ten hours, on an airline that only flies into this destination three times a week.

So you book the next flight out. You race to the airport the following day with the hope that you will make it there in time to see your loved one. You arrive for your international flight two and a half hours before departure, thinking you've allotted ample time to check in and board the plane.

You're met by an airline agent who tells you that no one else is being allowed on the flight and that the check-in gate has been closed. You have all kinds of questions racing through your mind as you battle to make sense of why they would close the departure gate so early.

Nothing you seem to say matters to this agent, and precious minutes are ticking away. You see the other waiting passengers being turned away, and you can't believe what's happening.

What are the immediate emotions you feel?

_____

_____

_____

What would you do about how you feel?

_____

_____

_____

This happened to me in March of 2003, as I was desperately trying to fly home to Ghana to see my father one last time. As incensed and frustrated as I felt about the whole situation, which I thought was beyond ridiculous, I contained my emotions and spoke to the ticket agents as politely as I could. (Everyone else was yelling.) I persisted, politely and respectfully, even as my twin brother and other distraught passengers gave up.

I knew this airline (my only choice for a direct flight) was grossly mismanaged. (On a side note, they went out of business just a few months later.) No matter what happened that day, I knew I needed to get my brother and me on that flight. After much pleading, in as calm and collected a voice as I could, we were both finally allowed to race onto the flight, even though we had to leave our luggage behind, to arrive with a later flight. I didn't care about that since my priority was seeing my father before he passed away.

Perhaps you're reading this and thinking, "I can relate to at least one of these situations." Or maybe you're thinking, "I've never had a situation where someone has botched an important online order or had to swim in a high-stakes race, or even had to rush to the bedside of a dying loved one."

Even if you can't relate to any of the above scenarios, I'm sure you can recall some situations in your past that tested your patience and resolve. *How did you feel and how did you respond?*

One thing will always remain true: While we *cannot* control what other people do or think, we *can* control our own emotions during our interactions with others, to influence the outcome in the best way possible. Understanding our emotions and what they're telling us is the first step to increasing our self-awareness.

Developing Self-Awareness

The road to greater self-awareness is an ongoing journey that requires us to use the tools we have at our disposal, to ensure that we're taking the time to more deeply understand ourselves and our reactions to everyday situations.

In much the same way that we cannot change what we don't acknowledge, we cannot manage our emotions if we don't first do the important work of better understanding ourselves.

Here are four ways to help you better understand yourself and your emotions.

Get Still

Most of us lead busy lives. In spite of this, we need to carve out five to ten minutes each day to be still. As you take this time to deliberately be still, ensure that you do it in a relatively quiet place away from noise and distractions.

Get still enough to notice your heart beat. Notice your in-and-out breaths. Think about the things you've done and get present with your feelings and your behavior throughout the day. Getting still allows you to enhance your self-awareness as you gain a deeper understanding of yourself and your emotions.

Document Your Day

Developing a healthy daily habit of writing in a journal can enhance your self-awareness. Even if you spend just five minutes a day doing this, the act of documenting your daily experiences will help you think more deeply and better understand your attitudes and reactions. Try it!

Analyze Your Emotional Triggers and Self-talk

Create a little time to sit down and think about your emotional triggers. Pay special attention to the things that set you off emotionally. Getting clear on what your emotional triggers are can help you alter the way you react to them in the future.

In this brief assessment below, consider the situations and circumstances that can trigger *your* emotions. It is important that you not only identify specific things that trigger you, it's also key to think about the "self-talk" that goes on in your mind immediately after you're triggered. Consider also jotting down some of the typical reactions you have as a result of being triggered and reflect on these.

Example Triggers:

- Insulted
- Feeling Patronized
- Not feeling treated fairly
- Interrupted
- Feeling left out

- Not feeling valued
- Chaos
- Feeling ignored
- Disapproval

Seek Out Feedback and Insight from Family, Friends, or Colleagues

The people closest to you in your personal and professional circles often know you best. Their input and insight into how they experience you can be invaluable.

Besides the fact that having others point out your weaknesses can be ego-bruising and even anxiety-producing, it can also feel uncomfortable to ask someone you know to reveal blind spots that they may have observed in you. Here's a suggestion of how to do it in a meaningful way.

I call it the "Tissue-Box Test."

Just as the name suggests, it involves an empty tissue box:

First, tape the box up so that you have just a thin opening somewhere on the box.

Then, on a separate small index card, write down between three to five questions that center around how others experience you. Suggested questions are: *What three words describe my temperament? What are three positive traits you see in me? When it comes to handling stress, how do you think I fare? What is one thing you think I could improve to make me a better person?*

Once they've completed their answers, ask them to fold their card up and drop it into the slit in the tissue box. Once you've gathered all the cards, you can open up the box and read them privately. Having them contribute their feedback anonymously is important and will give you the most transparent and honest perspective on your blind spots. After all, they're called "blind spots" because these are typically things about us that we can't see—or don't want to see. It is totally up to you to decide what you will internalize and commit to working on and what you will choose to ignore.

As we become more proficient at understanding our emotions and learning more about the things we can improve upon, we can then focus our attention on the matters that will help us better manage our emotions. Here are three strategies to help with managing emotions:

"Grow the Gap"

When triggered by something or someone, it's important to widen the gap between your impulse and your action. If, for instance, you receive a rude or condescending e-mail from a co-worker, your impulse might be to pick up the phone or send them a harsh reply with a few choice words.

Instead of acting on that negative impulse, however, try taking ten minutes to step away from it all. Put simply, "growing the gap," in this case, could buy you enough time to calm down and think more clearly.

When it comes to developing our EI, there's no doubt about it: Growing the gap between your impulse and action is essential. Failing to grow this gap prevents you from being able to avoid a mistake before it's been made. And everyone knows that, once you send that e-mail or utter that rude retort, the action cannot be undone.

Talk to Yourself

It's often been said that only people who have lost their minds are the ones who talk to themselves.

I say to heck with that theory!

When it comes to managing your emotions, I *encourage* you to talk to yourself—far more often than you probably already do.

This is a practice I find extremely helpful with calming my mind and allowing me to focus on what's most important in my interactions with others. I've found that if, for instance, I'm engaging in a challenging conversation with someone and they say something to me that feels insulting or uncalled-for, instead of spiraling out of control with negative self-talk, I simply stop myself and ask, "Is it possible they don't intend to be insulting or demeaning?"

I've learned that even if I don't know the honest answer to that question, or even if I feel that they meant it, asking that question pauses my mind. It "grows my gap," as it were.

It helps me focus away from personalizing things as much as I otherwise would. What do you say to yourself in those triggering moments that helps you defuse your mind to get clear-headed about what to do next?

Ask Gateway Questions

One of the most effective ways to manage your emotions is by asking yourself "Gateway" questions. In moments when you're feeling angry, frustrated or fearful, asking these types of questions can be very empowering and grounding.

Gateway questions essentially convert complaints you have in your mind into practical and productive questions that can energize you and orient you towards finding solutions to your challenges. They typically begin with the words *how* or *what*.

If you've been complaining and feeling dejected by the fact that you haven't been hired after months of job hunting, instead of asking yourself "Static" questions that are typically destructive and disempowering and begin with *why*, ask yourself a gateway question.

Instead of asking, "W*hy* hasn't anyone hired me yet?" you could instead ask, "*What* can I do to creatively enhance my marketability?"

This will focus your attention on problem-solving, which in turn will help keep you calmer and more clear-headed.

While the path to achieving greater self-awareness and self-mastery may not be easy or without some growing pains, it's a journey worth undertaking. Understanding your emotions and getting more skilled at managing their impact on you and others is a priceless asset. In the chapters that follow, we'll take a closer look at just how we benefit personally and professionally.

CHAPTER 3
Empathy and Relationship Management

"No one cares how much you know, until they know how much you care."
—Theodore Roosevelt

WHILE OUR FOCUS ON SELF-AWARENESS and self-mastery in the previous chapter had us looking inward, this chapter invites you to look outward by examining how cultivating true empathy helps you deepen the quality of your personal and professional relationships.

At the end of the day, you want to be happy and feel fulfilled. Right? If your answer is a resounding, "Yes!" then perhaps you agree with what positive psychologists have asserted: that the happiest people are those who have meaningful and sustained connections in their lives.

One of the most effective ways we develop more rewarding relationships is by being empathic towards others. Forging meaningful connections is a two-way street. When people feel that you *see* them, you *hear* them, and you understand what they're feeling, they open up and more easily create a bond with you.

Our need for love and belonging, based on Maslow's Third Hierarchy of needs, connects closely to our human need to be seen, to be appreciated and to be understood. This is exactly what others want from us and ultimately this is what empathy is all about.

It is an interpersonal skill that does not demand that we step into someone else's shoes perfectly; it just requires that we step into *them*. Empathy is simply making a valiant effort to see what others see and to imagine what they feel.

Of all the things that can act as an obstacle and prevent us from showing more empathy, one contributor stands out, and it has to do with the inaccurate assumptions we tend to make.

Before I began writing this book, I knew I didn't want it to read like a "boring" technical book. So instead, I decided to capture and convey the everyday experiences of people witnessing emotional intelligence at work in their lives. Little did I know that one of the most important lessons I would learn would come from an experience I personally had during my own research-gathering process.

In an effort to form as strong a foundation as I possibly could to create the underpinnings and structure for this book, I wanted to capture as many "human" stories as I could, so I decided to spend a few months as a Lyft driver, maneuvering through the streets of Washington, D.C.

Boy, did I get more stories than I bargained for! I was pleasantly surprised by how many folks were willing to share their experiences, and even more surprised by how many wanted me to use their stories in any way I saw fit. Many loved the idea that I was writing a book that focused on a topic (and a skillset) as important as emotional intelligence, which only confirmed, in my mind, that EI is much-needed in our world today.

Out of a few hundred rides, I had very pleasant experiences … except for one, which later and upon reflection proved to be a tremendously useful teaching lesson in empathy.

It was 6:42 on a cool fall morning last year, and my very first ride had me pick up a lady who lived just a few blocks from me. My navigation app indicated that I had arrived at the destination. It turns out, however, that the GPS was slightly incorrect and I ended up on a one-way street and could not back out. This meant the lady had to walk down the block, about 75 feet, to get to my car.

When she entered my car, she seemed incensed and frustrated; she ignored my polite greeting and sincere apology. We didn't exchange another word until I got near her place of work in Dupont Circle. Luckily for her, even though she had opted for a "shared" ride, which meant we could have stopped to pick up one or two other passengers, she got to ride alone and avoid any potential delays.

As I was preparing to pull up to her destination, which was 175 feet away, my GPS indicated that I turn left. In hindsight, I realize now, I should have instead made a complete U-turn a few feet earlier, but since it was so early in the morning and there were no cars behind me, I began to reverse slightly to correct my path.

In the middle of reversing, I was startled by the sound of intense huffing and puffing coming from the back seat.

She began yelling, "Just let me the hell out!"

I couldn't believe my ears and I didn't understand why she was so angry.

Something told me to turn back, look at her and just say, "I'm sorry," which is what I did. But she bolted out, slamming the door shut and storming away.

What happened next was something I did, that many of us might be guilty of doing without even realizing it. I began a ten-minute verbal tirade with myself, boldly and satisfyingly declaring that she was a horrible, friendless, human being who was probably disliked by her co-workers and obviously was a very lonely person.

After my rant was over and I was feeling less inflamed, a thought struck me: I had just made a bunch of negative assumptions about this woman who I didn't know beyond her first name!

Wasn't I the one teaching others about emotional intelligence? Well, I surely wasn't practicing what I preached in that moment. Fortunately, in a moment of clarity, I snapped myself out of my tirade, shifted my train of thought, and dug down deep, to a place where empathy and understanding existed. Immediately, my thoughts became more compassionate. More understanding. More empathetic. These were some of my thoughts:

What if she awoke this morning with really bad health news? What if she was on the receiving end of extreme verbal, physical or emotional abuse from her partner? What if she'd just been told that she was going to get laid off? What if her world had somehow just crumbled down around her?

I obviously didn't know if any of these scenarios had unfolded. Yes, I admit her angry tone triggered me, and while I'm not excusing the way she behaved in response to my error, what I do know with certainty is that when I made healthier, more empathetic assumptions about her—accurate or inaccurate—I was covered by a sense of calm. I was able to let go of what had happened, because I was no longer personalizing the incident.

Maybe she got to work and felt bad for her behavior, especially after my apology, but I guess we'll never know. Just in the same way I'll never know why she snapped the way she did. What I *do* know is that the emotion of empathy isn't something we get to demonstrate only in moments of convenience; we don't just get to show it when it feels most comfortable or when it's most convenient.

The truth of the matter is that we all make assumptions about others and about situations we find ourselves in. Nothing interferes more with our ability to empathize and connect with others than the negative assumptions we make.

We cannot possibly empathize with someone while judging them at the same time. Simply put, when you make negative assumptions about others, it makes it very difficult (if not impossible) to understand what they're feeling or thinking.

Our attempts at empathy may not always result in a harmonious connection with others, but it sure as heck goes a long way in influencing how they experience us.

Take a moment to reflect on a conversation or interaction you might have had that didn't go as well as desired. Can you remember the incident? As you think back, were there assumptions you made about the person or the situation that might have fanned the flames of discord or conflict?

While I believe that others have a role to play in influencing how we relate to them and them to us, we can still use our empathetic skills to increase the likelihood of a productive, positive interaction. We alone have the power to focus on what *we can* control. Showing empathy—in spite of how others behave towards us—is challenging, certainly, but it is also something that is well within our own control. It takes practice, discipline, awareness and a sense of purpose to get to this level, but it is a level which we can certainly attain.

For a long time, empathy has been an underrated and overlooked trait in the workplace. In some cases, there is a notable disconnect between employees and their leadership teams when it comes to how they view empathy in their business environment.

A 2018 study by Businessolver found that, "92% of CEOs reported their organization was empathic, but only 50% of employees say their CEO was empathic."

In spite of this disconnect, thankfully, more and more business leaders are understanding that they cannot build a culture of empathy without considering the factors that contribute to making their employees feel respected, valued, and appreciated. Things like showing an interest in who they are beyond what they can produce; and giving them opportunities for continued professional growth.

I strongly believe that when you take care of your employees first, they, in turn and as a result, will take care of your customers. When employees within the workplace feel heard, understood and valued, it creates a cyclical and highly motivating pattern in that those same employees will ensure that the customer also feels valued and appreciated.

Since we're living in a time when so much of the customer buying experience is based on how they feel they are being treated, empathy ought to matter a great deal to organizations serious about competing in the 21st century.

If you're in a leadership role of any kind within an organization, I invite you to think about how you show empathy to others on a daily basis. Is there more room for you to show those you work with and those you serve that they are more than just a number?

Here are a few questions to jumpstart your personal assessment on how you fare when it comes to showing empathy:

1. When a colleague is in need, do you offer to help them or do you tend to lay low in the hope that they'll get through it on their own?

2. Do you check in with your staff on their work satisfaction from time to time?

3. Do you take time to get to know others, no matter their level in your organization?

4. When you have to deliver tough or critical feedback, do you give thought to how to share it, or is your focus mostly on just letting them know?

5. Do you revel in the achievements of others, even if you yourself gain no benefit from their success?

6. What do you do to show your employees that you care about their happiness at work *and* beyond its walls?

7. Are you open to hearing the opinions of others, even if the person isn't high on your "likeable list?"

8. Do you tend to prioritize an employee's well-being over a business outcome?

9. Are you concerned that showing empathy to staff members at your level and below will be mistaken for weakness?

I encourage you to consider the above questions, even if you don't directly manage others. As long as you interact with individuals on a daily basis, checking in on some of these questions from time to time will help you look outward and ensure your empathy skills remain sharpened.

We're about to take a deeper dive into some of the ways that we can enhance our empathic skills, but before we do that, it's important to shed light on some truths about this critical EI skill.

We've already touched on the fact that empathy is not about "being nice" simply for the sake of being nice. Here are some additional truths worth noting:

Empathy is a Learned Behavior Requiring Consistent Practice

While some people may have the propensity to more accurately feel what others are feeling, most of us have to cultivate empathy with tools that can help us become more attune to the feelings of others.

It's not automatic, that we are born with an innate ability to see what others see, understand what they feel, and communicate our understanding to them in non-judgmental ways.

Developing effective listening skills goes a long way in helping us learn how to become more empathic. And I'm not talking about listening just to respond. I mean listening so that we truly hear what others are saying and not saying.

Showing Empathy is Not the Same as Showing Sympathy

Feeling sympathy for someone means you can identify with the circumstance they find themselves in. Even if you've never met the person, you can still sympathize with them if you can relate to their situation in one way or another.

You can indeed sympathize with someone and still be disconnected with how they are feeling. This is one of the ways sympathy differs greatly from empathy.

Example: You recently received a speeding ticket and you tell a friend about it. You're upset because of how much of a wrench it will throw in your monthly budget. Your friend may sympathize with you if they've also received a speeding ticket at some point. They may however, be unable to connect with how you're feeling about it (empathize) if they happen to be very wealthy and are able to pay their ticket in the blink of an eye.

Simply put, empathy builds connection with others, while sympathy does not, because empathy is about identifying with how others feel and actually feeling those feelings ourselves. Neuroscientists often use this distinction: sympathy is feeling *for* someone, and empathy involves feeling *with* them.

Empathy is About Communicating in Non-judgmental Ways

In an effort to feel *with* someone else, it's vital that you become more mindful of your choice of words, most especially in moments when it feels least convenient to invest time and effort in finding the right words to say. Consider developing the habit of communicating in ways that convey understanding and not judgement.

Let's say your friend recently lamented to you about missing an international flight. A judgmental response would be, "I'm sorry you missed your flight. I typically get to the airport three hours ahead to avoid that."

An empathic response would be, "I'm sorry to hear that. You must feel really frustrated and inconvenienced."

Even if you think it was their fault, there's a time and place to address that. Just not in a moment when all they needed was a listening ear.

Empathic language goes a long way in helping us connect more deeply with others. This is language that clearly communicates that you have them in mind and understand their pain.

Here are additional examples of empathic phrases. Perhaps you could consider incorporating them into your own EI lexicon:

"I understand how this must make you feel."

"I wish I could have been with you in that moment."

"You're making total sense."

"That would upset me as well."

It also makes a world of difference to also use empathic language in your written communications to others.

You Don't Have to Agree with Someone to Empathize with Them

How can you "feel with" someone else if you can't even agree with them or their perspective? Simply acknowledging how someone else feels doesn't mean you have to agree with them or even take responsibility for what they are feeling.

You show empathy by giving them room to share their story and what they're feeling and you listen intently with an ear of understanding not an ear of agreement. It's important to remember that showing empathy has nothing to do with trying to say things just to make someone feel better. You're simply trying to allow them to share their story so they feel heard and understood.

You Can Suffer from Showing Too Much Empathy

Yes, you heard that right. Having too much empathy is possible for some people. It doesn't have to be a bad thing if it is managed properly. Some people are naturally highly sensitive and highly intuitive towards others. This causes their emotional antennas to extend beyond just understanding how someone else feels, and to being fully absorbed in other people's feelings.

If you identify with this, you may be losing yourself deep in the feelings of others, which can be exhausting, toxic and even leave you with feelings of guilt and frustration for the pain and discomfort that others feel.

So what can you to do to free yourself from this emotional congestion, if you happen to be one of these people? Whenever you feel burdened by the weight of other people's emotions, it's important to get really *present* with what you are feeling.

Consciously take over and guide your self-talk and become aware of the conversation you're having in your mind.

Consider this self-talk as a valuable EI tool to help you reign things in: "I know I'm someone who feels deeply for others. I care greatly about being there for others and the only way I can continue to be present is to first take care of myself. While I know I'm a nurturer, it doesn't make me a bad person to step away for much-needed self-care."

Earlier in the chapter, I promised that we would look at various ways to grow our empathic abilities, so let's jump right in and focus on four in particular.

Challenge Yourself to Step into the Shoes of Others Often

Sometimes empathizing with someone else can feel uncomfortable or even difficult, especially if you don't feel like you have the perfect thing to say to make them feel better. Remember that empathy isn't about perfection. It's about making an honest effort to listen and connect with what someone is saying and feeling.

An important consideration in "stepping into someone else's shoes" is to realize that we literally have to step out of our own shoes first. There's a reason the expression doesn't say, "Put one foot in their shoe while keeping the other in yours."

If we look at the migrant refugee crisis happening off the shores of Europe, it is easy to sympathize with those escaping in unsuitable boats and rafts. However, many observers don't understand why people would risk their lives and travel in such treacherous conditions.

Only when you imagine yourself living in some of the extremely challenging and life-threatening circumstances that they have to live in each day, can you begin to truly feel empathy for them and understand why they risk everything for the chance of a better existence elsewhere.

Enhance Your Listening Skills and Ability to Stay in the Present Moment

The art of true listening is something that eludes most of us, because often times we are distracted by our own thoughts and by what we want to say next.

Commit to practicing active listening, which will redirect your focus from being inside your own head, to being present and engaged in what someone else is telling you. Ask yourself questions like, "Am I truly listening, or just waiting my turn to talk?" "Am I hearing something they're not openly expressing?"

Echo some of what you hear them saying as a sign that you are paying attention and you understand what they're feeling. Sometimes simply listening without judgement (or without comment) is enough to show empathy towards others.

Examine Your Assumptions

Previously, I mentioned that when we assume things about others, it makes it difficult to understand or appreciate their perspective or their feelings. When someone opens up to you about an issue or concern they have, as you listen to them, ask yourself if you're forming any negative assumptions about them or what they're saying.

Empathizing with others asks that we imagine what others are feeling and this can sometimes open us up to make assumptions. We just need to pay attention to whether we're making healthy or negative assumptions and drop any negative ones.

Avoid Projecting as a Way to Connect with Others

When trying to show empathy, we must resist the urge to attempt to match their pain or discomfort.

For example, a co-worker tells you they got passed up for a promotion. You can see their heartbreak and disappointment. You say, "That's horrible. You know this is the second time I have been passed up for a promotion. Don't worry; it's their loss."

In your attempt to "relate" to them, to let them know they're not alone, you inadvertently stole the spotlight from them by injecting yourself into the conversation. This oversight can derail your genuine effort to connect with them. Consider saying something like this instead, "I'm so sorry to hear that. I know how hard you worked for it. Do you want to talk about it?"

The one thing we know for sure is what it feels like to be on the receiving end of empathy. We know how we feel in the company of someone who's taken time to see us, hear us and understand how we feel. Doesn't it make sense for us to reciprocate that feeling for others, no matter what we get back in return? No one expects us to "do empathy perfectly." All that matters is that we try.

It is indeed true that the happiest people are those who have meaningful connections in their lives and empathy plays a major role in making that possible. Let's continue on this journey to better understand *why* it's so important to care about using emotional intelligence to manage your impact on others.

SECTION TWO

WHY CARE?

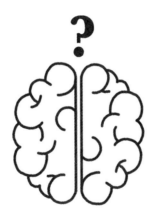

CHAPTER 4
Your Personal Growth Depends on It

*"There is only one corner of the universe you can be
certain of improving...and that's your own self."*
−Aldous Huxley

ALMOST TWO DECADES AGO ON a Sunday evening, there I was, in the back of the restaurant where I was employed, dutifully rolling silverware into crisp white napkins as part of my required prep work for the next morning's shift. I was minding my own business in relative calm when suddenly, I heard our manager yelling out instructions at the top of his lungs.

"Get into the damn dining room now and move the #*%$* furniture, and *don't* let me ask you again!" he bellowed.

Then as fast as he stormed in, he slithered back into his office.

If you had been with me in the restaurant earlier that day, during the brunch shift, you would have understood how this all began. Here's how the scenario unfolded:

Customarily, a few servers who worked the first Sunday-of-the-month dinner shift had to move approximately 120 heavy wooden chairs and tables out of the main dining room so that the carpet could be professionally cleaned.

On most occasions, our general manager (GM) would give us some extra money as compensation, since this fairly heavy manual labor was beyond the scope of what we were required to do as servers. We would, in turn, share some of that same money with the busboys helping us. They were always happy to earn some extra money and we were happy to have the extra help after a long Sunday shift.

On this fateful day, however, the restaurant manager refused to ask the GM for money to compensate us and each time we gently asked him, he rudely brushed us off and insisted that we call the owners and ask them ourselves (delivered with a few expletives).

This manager had a "reputation." He reveled in bullying and bluster, and he was notorious for mistreating servers and bartenders, so much so that observant customers, on a few occasions, complained to the GM about his behavior.

Even as I quietly rolled silverware that evening, an anger had been brewing inside me from the time he began his verbal assaults during our earlier brunch shift. The final straw was that moment he barged in yelling and threatening us one last time.

Something snapped inside me.

It felt like an out-of-body experience as I tossed aside the rolled silverware. I was filled with rage—no, make that *overflowing* with rage—as I bulldozed my way through to the main dining room and commanded my fellow servers to move out of the way.

Judging by the seriousness of my tone, they obliged and promptly stepped aside. I began hurling chairs through the open doors with the force and aggression of a discus thrower vying for a gold medal at the Olympic Games. I even threw some chairs overhead into the next room where we were supposed to neatly stack them.

I had come completely undone and as I surrendered to my rage, I even broke a few chairs. My co-workers looked at me in jaw-dropping disbelief. They had never seen me act that way. In truth, I had never seen *myself* act that way. No one said a word about it to the manager that night.

I calmed down once I left the restaurant and was immediately consumed by a strong gust of guilt and shame. In my rage and frustration, I could have shattered the glass doors or seriously injured someone (or myself). Amidst the guilt and shame, questions swirled furiously in my mind: *How could I behave like that? Hadn't my parents raised me to be far more controlled than that? What had happened, exactly, to cause such a serious snap in my own protocol? My dear father would have been rolling in his grave!*

The next morning, I promptly went to the GM's office and assured him that if there were any broken chairs amongst the stacks, I would certainly pay for the damage; after all, it was my fault for throwing them so aggressively.

The irony is that I was planning on quitting my job in three weeks, primarily because of that manager. I fully expected to get fired on the spot and was surprised by the GM's calm and compassionate tone. I told him that I was deeply embarrassed for allowing myself to act like a crazed animal and that I could no longer work for a manager who brought the worst out in me.

Because I was one of their top servers, the GM suggested that I take a couple of weeks off to refresh my mind. I thanked him for his kind offer, but I declined and tendered my resignation that afternoon: What I did was inexcusable and I needed to change my environment immediately.

Upon reflection, I realize that in that regrettable moment, my humanity was confiscated by my inability to manage my emotions. And whether I was conscious of it or not at the time, my actions were *still* within my control.

What I also needed to realize was that sometimes exercising emotional intelligence requires us to recognize when an environment has become toxic enough for us to make an exit.

In the blink of an eye, I had become a living, breathing example of what happens when we allow our emotions to get the best of us. While that was a deeply embarrassing and shameful moment in my life, and while I certainly regret my behavior that day, I do *not* regret the opportunity it gave me to deeply self-reflect and commit to being a better human being.

The bottom-line lesson I learned was this: We don't grow personally in times of comfort and convenience. If you think about it, what personal growth really happens when our lives are "peachy" and cushioned by the cozy conveniences of our safe, secure comfort zones?

For as much as we have days ahead of us, we will continue to encounter moments that will test our resolve and our ability to manage our emotions. We will fail, time and time again, to grow personally, if we don't take time to understand our own emotions and their impact on us and others.

Simply defined, *personal growth is a lifelong commitment to the constant practice of absorbing our life experiences in a way that allows us to improve our habits, choices, behavior and reactions. This is what emotional intelligence is all about.*

We all know that life is constantly offering up challenges, crises and curve balls. It's ultimately up to us whether we choose to learn and grow from these challenges or remain uninspired and unchanged by the experiences of our lives.

I believe it was Oprah who said it best in *The Harvard Gazette,* when the newspaper excerpted from her commencement speech to the Class of 2013: "There really *is* only one goal in life, and that is this: To fulfill the highest, most truthful expression of yourself as a human being. You want to max out your humanity by using your energy to lift yourself up, your family, and the people around you."

This in a nutshell, is the essence of personal growth.

Personal growth, as its name implies, is something that happens inside of us. It is an intentional path we decide to take with no final destination. We don't get to arrive at some terminal called "Personal Growth Once and for All."

Our lives are constantly changing and evolving and we need to enhance our ability to be great observers of the changes and evolutions. We need to learn all that we can along the way; these learning experiences will ultimately help us progress towards our full potential as human beings.

When I think about the vital relationship between our personal growth and our ability to manage our emotions and their impact on others, I'm reminded of something that once happened to my grandmother's friend.

It was April 8th, 1968, and she was transiting through London's Heathrow airport. She was scheduled to depart on a British Overseas Airways flight and she had a three-hour wait. Because she had been travelling for many hours and didn't get much sleep on her previous flight, she decided to take a nap in the waiting lounge. Before she did, she asked a passenger sitting nearby to wake her up when it was time to board the flight.

She tried to make herself as comfortable as one possibly could on those not-so-comfortable hard, plastic airport chairs. About an hour into her wait, she fell into a deep slumber. When she awoke, she was alarmed and disheartened to realize that the person she asked to wake her up did not. Apparently, the gate agents had also called her name three times and she didn't respond.

As she sprung up from her chair, she turned to look outside the window and saw what she believed was her departing flight, taxiing slowly out onto the runway. She began yelling and screaming at the gate agents and anyone in her vicinity, in total disbelief (and rage) that no one had bothered to wake her up. She was deeply incensed and beside herself, because she now had to wait even longer to try to get another connecting flight to Zurich.

She was inconsolable; nothing the agents said to her made her feel any better. Just a few minutes into her outburst, the gate agents got word that shortly after the plane took off, it suffered an engine failure and caught fire. The pilot pulled off a miraculous emergency landing two and half minutes after take-off. In spite of best efforts, five people on the plane lost their lives.

It turns out that my grandmother's friend's seat was supposed to be in the middle of the plane where it caught fire. With this reality, she sunk to the ground in utter disbelief, filled to the brim with embarrassment for the way she acted towards people around her … and profound gratitude for the fact that her own life had been spared.

As she apologized profusely for her behavior, she was overcome by an overwhelming sense of guilt and shame; she survived by simply missing her flight, yet others had been badly injured and even killed.

She was never the same after that. Who would be? In her case, she was changed for the better, because she previously had a reputation of being a pretty grumpy old lady who never seemed happy or content.

To say that that was a time of personal growth for her would be an understatement. It was a profound deepening of her sense of gratitude and a renewed awareness that her emotions would never, ever get the best of her again.

While her story is most certainly one about second chances, it also serves as a vital lesson in the importance of making an effort when it comes to managing our emotions and fully realizing the impact we have on those around us.

Another important connection is between our personal growth and the perspectives we take on.

A few years ago, I found myself standing in the checkout line at Trader Joe's in Alexandria, Virginia. When my turn arrived at the checkout counter, I began placing my items on the counter.

My cashier was a lovely, bubbly, elderly lady, who I had seen many times before, but had never spoken to. By all accounts, she appeared to love her work and the opportunity to brighten someone else's day with a few jokes or kind compliments.

As she grabbed my bottle of Cabernet Sauvignon, she paused and politely asked for my identification card to prove that I was old enough to buy the wine. I chuckled at her request and in addition to complaining a little about still being carded, I said, "Don't my grey hairs pass for proof that I'm over 21?"

She looked at me, angled her eye glasses halfway down the bridge of her nose like your grandmother would, and dished me a mouthful of wisdom, saying, "Honey, you shouldn't ever complain about your grey hairs. They are a privilege. I tell my son all the time that the only alternative to growing old is dying young."

Talk about learning a powerful lesson in putting things in perspective!

There is so much rich learning that happens when we're committed to personal growth and development and I wanted to capture other people's perspectives and motivations for wanting to improve upon their own humanity.

Numerous conversations I've had with friends and colleagues have led me to include some excerpts from their insightful feedback. The question I asked them was this: "Do you care about your personal growth and about trying to be a better human being? If so, why do you care?"

What I found interesting in what folks told me is that they could respond to my question with an immediate and resounding "Yes, I care!" They were, however, much more challenged by me asking *why*. They had to dig a little deeper for that answer. I think it is a question we ought to ask ourselves more often in order to take inventory of how we're doing in the personal growth department.

After you read through the excerpts that follow, I invite you to pause and reflect on your own reasons for why you care about your personal growth. What does it mean to you and why do you stay committed to the journey?

Excerpt 1

"I care about my personal growth because I feel the happiest and most alive when I know that I am evolving as a human being. I see life as a long learning process to create a better version of myself in order to be a better wife/ mother/ daughter/ friend/ community member. I think how you treat others is the most important thing in life and when you are happy with yourself, being kind/helpful to others becomes more natural."

Excerpt 2

"I have to be about growth because it's the only tool that carves new paths for doing the 'old' better and more efficiently than before, and equally creating the 'new' with less fear and more joy than my current mindset allows."

Excerpt 3

"I care about growing into a more compassionate, and loving human being for the joy of it. I am my most happy self when I am practicing kindness and compassion. With so many examples of atrocities in this life, one doesn't need to look far to find light—it's within and it takes practice."

Excerpt 4

"There's so much going on around us that is negative, I'd like to have a positive impact, no matter how big or small, on those I come in contact with. People are stressed the hell out all the time now. Even in doing things that are supposed to be fun or good. So, if working to be a better human being can add even the smallest joy to someone else, then why not?"

Excerpt 5

"Gosh—without personal growth, we may as well crawl into a tortoiseshell and disappear. Building on self-awareness, recognizing our strengths and weaknesses, and just being a decent human being is so socially crucial.

Whenever there's conflict, argument or things aren't working out, I take a step back to evaluate—what should I have done differently? I solicit feedback from others as well. I don't believe you're stuck with a personality. Negative aspects can be shredded and positive ones learned."

Excerpt 6

"I care about personal growth and the idea of being a better human being. The world is changing every day and in order to stay relevant and be a productive citizen, I think you have to push and challenge yourself to find ways to grow.

Personal growth to me means daily learning through actions that allow my mind/body to have new experiences. While the core of a person can always remain, it's never too late to find ways to grow in areas you never thought. I think the beauty of personal growth is that it allows you to appreciate growing older. I care about growing personally because it makes me feel more alive and in sync with the world around me."

Excerpt 7

"Every day we exist within this world, we add to the compendium of our individual experiences. In theory, this journey is one that leads us toward our best, enlightened selves, and I believe that personal growth is a commitment to progress. However, progress is a pendulum, and like a pendulum, one's progress is not predictable. Progress is individual, and progress is customized, but progress is not linear."

In the space below, jot down your personal reasons *why* you care about your own personal growth. Articulate as best you can, what it means to you and why you stay committed to the personal growth journey.

_____

_____

_____

Before I asked others for some of the insights you just read, I needed to get clear on my own reasons for caring about personal growth. One of the reasons that came to mind can best be explained through something I experienced when I turned forty.

My husband asked me what I wanted to do to celebrate my milestone birthday. He suggested, among other things, an overseas trip or a very special, romantic dinner out.

None seemed to excite me as much as the idea of having my closest friends over to our place for a party. (Side note: We were always known to throw legendary parties. I imagined this one being much the same and I couldn't think of a better way to ring in a new decade than to be surrounded by people I cared most about.)

As predicted, the party did not disappoint. We had the pleasure of indulging in a sinfully good time with a house full of about forty-five friends. I even got a heartwarming treat, having my dear cousin surprise me by flying all the way from London to help us celebrate.

A couple of my friends went to great lengths to conspire with my twin brother, who lived in Senegal, to have him send as many childhood photos of me as he could. They then painstakingly put a marvelous album together chronicling the past four decades of my life and asked those in attendance to jot down a few sentiments about me.

I was absolutely blown away by the things I read, and was brought to tears by the realization of what they thought of me and what our connection meant to them. Their shared sentiments touched me deeply and made me realize, all over again, how good it feels to know that others value you and experience you in positive ways.

My hope, as I open up that beautiful album each year, is that I continue to cherish their words and work hard to earn the reputation of being fun-spirited, generous, compassionate and kind.

Before I completed this writing project, I was asked whether I felt that my personal growth had been enhanced by writing this book.

After pondering for a few moments, I answered with a resounding, "Yes!" Yes, it's totally enhanced my personal growth, because writing this book has allowed me to reflect back on my own life experiences. I got a chance to look at these experiences from a different angle, a different lens, a different perspective, and try to give them meaning that could be universal and useful for others. Perhaps even more important than the opportunity to reflect is the opportunity to share and, hopefully, inspire my readers in a way that will facilitate their own growth, heighten their sense of self-awareness and hone their mastery over their emotions.

At the end of the day, when we consider the alternative to personal growth, it makes complete sense to commit to a path of continued development. Deciding not to grow personally is essentially opening a door to isolation, loneliness and despair. If we want to feel like we matter and that our presence makes a difference, a commitment to personal growth has to be a priority.

In the next chapter, we will look at the role emotional intelligence plays in our professional growth and development. So let's take all that we have learned in this chapter and step into the next chapter fully prepared for yet another deep dive!

CHAPTER 5
Your Professional Growth Depends on It

"The greatest ability in business is to get along
with others and influence their actions."
– John Hancock

ON MANY OCCASIONS, I WAS privileged to witness first-hand the beneficial impact of emotional intelligence on professional growth, by observing my father's professional career.

In my youth, I never quite understood how we were afforded the opportunity to live in a different country every few years. While some might think moving this much had its disadvantages, I welcomed the opportunity to explore other countries, learn new languages, and make new friends, even as I missed my old ones.

My father, Eric Baffour, was an extremely talented, skilled, and sought-after development officer who worked for development banks in various countries throughout Africa. His work focused on helping local communities with development projects designed to enhance their everyday lives in one way or another.

In Madagascar, for instance, he worked on projects that brought vital funding to fruit and poultry farmers to help them maximize the efficiency with which they brought their produce to market. In the Comoros Islands, he helped secure resources for small-scale fish farming, which provided a vital safety net to disadvantaged groups who were able to rely on this as a source of employment.

What I came to realize, over the years, was that my father left an indelible impression on everyone with whom he worked, in every country we lived. Many of his colleagues never forgot how his immense talents helped catapult them towards success. My father improved the lives of many, enriched the lives of many, and perhaps even *saved* the lives of many.

He was quick to give praise and allow others on his team to take the spotlight for successful projects that he spearheaded. While his colleagues leaned on him for his expertise and industry knowledge, they also paid close attention to how well he treated everyone with whom he came into contact, whether you were the hotel maid or the Agency Director.

He often invited colleagues over to our home for dinner as they passed through en route to another country. Conversations enjoyed over bowls brimming with succulent pot roasts and mouthwatering side dishes, lovingly prepared by my mother, gave me and my brothers a front-row seat. Time and time again, we witnessed just how "amazingly cool" our father was in the eyes of those who worked with him.

Every few years, as his work contract approached an end, my father's phone wouldn't stop ringing with calls coming in from people who knew him, suggesting new work opportunities for him to consider in other countries. And usually, off we went, ready to explore another land.

Even though I lost my father in 2003, his spirit continues to shine. In fact, I had a touching full-circle moment just a few months ago that reminded me just how much he impacted others with his bright and brilliant presence. It happened right after a keynote presentation I'd delivered to five hundred IT professionals from around the world, who'd convened at the World Bank in Washington, D.C.

At the end of my presentation, a gentleman came up to me and asked, "Is Eric Baffour your father?" His question caught me by surprise and yet I was so very pleased (and proud!) to hear someone I didn't know, from the other side of the world, mention my father's name.

As it turned out, his name was John and he'd worked with my father in Rwanda right until my father had to leave the country because of the genocide in 1994.

Warm feelings of nostalgia coursed through my veins as John shared his fondest memories working with my father in Kigali. It was as if Daddy was physically present in the room with us that morning.

While Daddy's legacy lives on, deep in the hearts and minds of everyone who crossed paths with him, he forever remains a powerful example in emotional intelligence, bringing truth to the fact that what we do and what we know in life is certainly important, but the depth of our character and our ability to create, transform and strengthen the emotions of others is ultimately what matters *most*.

As we steer through our professional journeys, leveraging the emotional intelligence skills of self-awareness, self-mastery and empathy will ensure that we are able to peak perform when it comes to a range of things, including job interviews, critical team collaboration, conflict resolution, navigating difficult conversations, and so much more.

It is no secret that our cognitive intelligence, more commonly known as IQ, plays an important role in our professional success. It is, however, not the sole contributing factor in determining how we advance professionally. In some situations, having high EI matters *more* than IQ, especially when navigating the sometimes-delicate interactions with others.

In the fall of 2007, I took on a three-year role as Regional Director for a national educational sales firm. In that time, I delivered approximately 630 presentations on the do's and don'ts of the college planning process to eager high school students and their parents.

Following each presentation, families interested in learning more about the college planning process could stay behind to be interviewed by my team of educational sales consultants. Students who qualified through our interview process then had the option to invest in coaches to help them further.

Aside from my role of presenting pertinent information to these audiences, I occasionally interviewed, recruited, and hired individuals to join our travelling sales team.

On paper, a fair number of these people exhibited similar traits, qualifications and skill levels. I used my best judgment to hire people with good interpersonal skills who I thought would be a valuable addition to the team.

After a few weeks of travelling to various cities on the East Coast with my team, I noticed that one particular team member, Andrea, was beginning to exhibit undesirable behavior. I observed mounting friction between her and other team members. She also began to show up late and didn't contribute as often as she should have with administrative tasks.

On one occasion, I overheard the tail end of a conversation in which she berated a parent because he was uncomfortable making a financial commitment without his wife being present. After her outburst, I pulled her aside to let her know how highly inappropriate her behavior was.

Her actions gave me no choice but to put her on probation. This meant that she would have one last chance to step up and be a better, more respectful team member—or else she had to leave the team. This ultimatum was a big deal; it represented a major potential shift because out of approximately ten consultants that I worked with on any given weekend, she was by far the top performer.

Fast-forward a month later, and sadly, she continued to butt heads with people on the team and demonstrate less than desirable behavior, *even though she maintained a high individual sales performance.* The long and short of the issue was this: she was meeting (and even exceeding) her numbers … but doing very little to contribute to the larger collective team tasks.

I had to let her go.

Everyone on the team was shocked to see her get terminated, because they thought her top-performer status rendered her immune from adverse consequences. It appeared that Andrea herself assumed that because she was such a superstar revenue earner, she was indispensable.

She was sorely mistaken.

Following this incident, my team came to realize that while I certainly valued strong sales performance, having a team of motivated, emotionally aware individuals—individuals who cared about the impact that they had on others—was far more important.

The bottom line is that our professional growth does indeed depend on how emotionally intelligent we are. Andrea's inability to manage her weaknesses and get along with others contributed to her downward spiral and ultimately cost her job and her significant income.

And here, a teachable moment that I will encapsulate like this: *While your talent and skills can most certainly get you "in the door," it will be your ability to manage your emotions and their impact on you and others that will truly make you an invaluable asset.*

A recent Harvard study revealed that when technical skills and IQ are roughly the same, it is EI that accounts for nearly 90% of what moves people up the ladder. Similar sentiments have been echoed by a leading online employment website, CareerBuilder, which states that, "71% of hiring managers say that they put a higher value on EI than they do on IQ."

This begs the question: *Why are companies placing such a premium on retaining and seeking out employees with high emotional intelligence?* The following five reasons shed light on why emotionally intelligent people are in such high demand.

As you read through these reasons, I invite you to pause and reflect on how you can also harness these in-demand emotional intelligence qualities for your own benefit:

They are Empathetic

We all know someone who has reached a height in their career because of their IQ or technical abilities, but were hampered in advancing further because they lacked empathy skills. Empathy is essentially the core of relationship management and people who genuinely listen to others (even when they disagree) are able to navigate successfully through conflicts and positively influence others.

As our world becomes increasingly global and diverse, companies know that they benefit greatly by having individuals on board who can get along well with people of varying backgrounds, cultures, mindsets, and philosophies.

Here, let's take a momentary pause for reflection and self-study. Think about an interaction or situation in your professional career where the outcome wasn't what you intended or hoped for. Knowing what you know now about the power of EI, how could you have leveraged empathy skills to steer things towards a different outcome?

_____

_____

_____

They Engage Pressure Productively

Emotionally intelligent people distinguish themselves by their ability to manage their emotions in the most challenging circumstances. Take an air traffic controller, for example: If you've ever flown on an airplane, then you've benefitted from the high-stress, no-room-for-error work performed by air traffic controllers who collaborate constantly with your pilot to guide your plane safely to the ground.

While some professions are high-stakes, pressure-inducing and almost unbearably demanding, we can all (no matter the profession) benefit by increasing our ability to master our emotions and reactions to tense situations. It's not difficult to see why having a firm and steady handle on your emotions during stressful times is an asset that companies value.

Let's take another pause here for reflection and self-study:

Think about a situation in your professional career that felt more overwhelming and stressful than you would have liked. Knowing what you know now about self-awareness and self-mastery, how could you have managed your emotions differently?

_____

_____

_____

They Collaborate Effectively and Positively Influence Others

People with a heightened ability to get along with others and positively impact, control and guide their own behavior are invaluable assets, especially to companies who depend on solid team cohesion in order to achieve business results.

Highly emotionally intelligent people have well-developed people skills that allow them to build meaningful relationships with diverse groups of people, and companies value this kind of contribution.

Again, let's dive deeper with a moment of reflection and self-examination:

Think about a challenging situation where you failed to collaborate with others to get something done or win them over. Knowing what you know now about the power of EI, how could you have leveraged EI skills to steer things towards a different, more positive outcome?

_____

_____

_____

They Embrace and Deliver Feedback in Healthy Ways

Anyone looking to better themselves certainly understands the importance of being open to receiving feedback, even when that feedback is focused on things in need of improvement. How else can we grow personally or professionally if we aren't continuously working to improve ourselves?

Because emotionally intelligent people have a high self-regard rooted in an understanding that they are not infallible, they are able to tame their ego and absorb feedback far more productively than the ego-driven, emotionally unaware individual.

A lot of employee morale within companies hinges on how individuals interact with one another and how they grow to trust each other. People with high EI are able to use their self-awareness and empathy skills to communicate feedback to others in ways that inspire positive action; this is a highly marketable and, thus, a highly desirable skill to possess, worthy enough to be sought after and retained.

Let's take a momentary deep dive again:

Think about a difficult or challenging interaction in which you had to either give or receive feedback; perhaps that feedback might even have been negative. Knowing what you know now about the power of EI, how could you have leveraged EI skills to steer things towards a more productive outcome?

_____

_____

_____

They Tend to be More Thoughtful and Deliberate in Their Decision-Making

We make decisions every day of our lives and research has shown that our emotions drive a lot of the decision-making process. People who have an inability to manage their emotions are at the mercy of making impulsive and ill-thought-out decisions. Put simply, they are far more vulnerable and, thus, far more susceptible to failure.

Companies value individuals who manage their emotions when thinking through critical tasks; they place a well-deserved premium on those employees who make good judgments about the impact of their decisions and actions on others.

And here, a final pause for reflection and self-examination:

Think about a challenging decision you had to make either by yourself or within a team that didn't quite produce the outcome you desired. Knowing what you know now about the power of EI, how could you have used emotional management and empathy skills to steer things towards a better outcome?

_____

_____

_____

In addition to the above reasons that increase your visibility, value and marketability in the workplace, possessing high emotional intelligence ultimately ensures that you're able to have more harmonious and productive work relationships.

While I admit that there are times when we may interact with someone who is just plain negative and difficult no matter what, there are many more times we consciously or unconsciously play a role in conflict situations that arise in the workplace.

Something I heard recently reminded me of this. It happened during a conversation I had with a client as part of a research-gathering session before an important keynote presentation.

While Karen and I were chatting about some of the changes unfolding within her organization, at one point, she became surprisingly personal. She began telling me about an experience with a co-worker with whom she'd had a very tough time getting along.

Karen was the kind of employee who did her best to inject a little fun and heartfelt humor into a sometimes-boring work space. She was always the one creating special recognition moments for staff birthdays and special occasions; during celebrations like St. Patrick's Day and Cinco De Mayo Day, for instance, she would lead the way with holiday-inspired decorations, and thoughtful, thematic ideas.

Everyone in her department welcomed and appreciated her enthusiasm and efforts, except one person: Debbie. Karen felt that Debbie unfairly criticized and constantly disapproved of every idea she came up with.

One day it happened: Karen hit her breaking point. She'd reached her saturation point and had had enough of Debbie's "sour" energy. She finally complained to her boss about the difficulties she was having interacting with Debbie.

To her grand surprise, Karen's boss suggested the unthinkable by uttering the following words: "Why don't you take her out to lunch and get to know her better?"

What? Karen couldn't believe her disappointed ears.

This, of course, was the absolute last thing Karen would have wanted. If anything, she wanted to find ways to minimize her interaction with Debbie.

"What an absurd idea," she thought to herself, but reluctantly, she agreed to take her nemesis out to lunch. As they ate, they made small talk. Debbie asked her questions about her family and Karen in turn did the same. In the middle of being asked about her family, Debbie burst into tears and Karen was taken aback. She couldn't understand—or stop—the unexpected flow of Debbie's tears.

A minute later, she learned that Debbie's 17-year-old daughter had committed suicide four weeks earlier and Debbie had lost her mother to cancer earlier in the year. As she sobbed uncontrollably, she confessed that she was having a really hard time coping and apologized to Karen for exhibiting such negative and pessimistic behavior around the office.

When Karen got back to work that afternoon, she was overcome with emotion, feeling embarrassed (and more than a little ashamed) because she'd had no earthly idea the challenges Debbie had been facing. Her newfound understanding allowed her to feel compassion for Debbie and they both resolved to make a greater effort to communicate in a healthier manner.

Karen realized that she had allowed Debbie's treatment of her to get the best of her emotions, in turn making her an active participant in their hostile work relationship. Since their lunch encounter, however, the two have become closer than ever and collaborate frequently on various office initiatives.

It's eye-opening to think that if Karen's boss hadn't urged her to have a lunch conversation with Debbie, they would still be at odds, making each other's lives at work more challenging than necessary.

It's fair to say that not every difficult interaction we have with others will result in a "Kumbaya moment," but every challenging interaction presents us with an opportunity to use our emotional intelligence skills to more effectively manage our emotions and connect with others.

After hearing Karen's story, I thought about all the times we encounter situations that escalate uncontrollably into conflict. The truth of the matter is that conflicts are inescapable and are bound to happen to all of us. I say this because conflicts happen between people, and people are filled with complex emotions.

Trying to escape conflict or avoid it is not the answer. *How we handle those dicey and challenging situations is ultimately what counts and emotional intelligence is indeed a vital skillset we can harness to help us successfully navigate through conflict.*

Can you think of a situation or an encounter in your own work life that resulted in some sort of conflict? *What was the incident? How did it escalate? What, if anything, could you have done differently to alter the course of the conflict or address it in a more productive manner?*

_____

_____

_____

As we wind down this chapter, I want you to give specific thought to this question: In your personal and professional circles, would you like to be known as someone who is level-headed, measured and successful at managing your emotions and teaching others to do the same? If you said "Yes," then having that reputation would make you highly emotionally intelligent.

Maybe you're like most of us who hesitate to give it a resounding "Yes," simply because you know that there is more work to be done to ensure you are fully deserving of that reputation. If you agree with this, I invite you to take a challenge with me.

It is a challenge that has certainly helped me improve my daily practice of being more aware of my own emotions and the impact they have on others around me. And it's a challenge that has the potential to inspire a new way of being and a new way of thinking, providing you embrace it fully.

To better explain it, I'd like to first take you on a brief detour and focus your attention on two of the world's most recognizable athletes: World-famous runner Usain Bolt and gold-medal gymnast Simone Biles.

Many know Usain Bolt as the winner of numerous Olympic gold medals and the current world record holder in the 100m and 200m sprints, and Simone Biles as the 2016 Olympic gold medal gymnast in the vault exercise, floor exercise and individual all-around events.

When we look back someday, over the span of history, they will both have a rightful place as one of the best in the world at what they did.

Long before either of them became gold medalists, however, they had to develop, nurture and exhibit particular behavior and habits. Achieving this world class status would have required them to be very mindful of matters large and small, such as the kind of food they consumed, the level of difficulty and frequency of their training sessions, their ability to sustain and recover from injury, and the decisions that drove their social, emotional and even creative proclivities.

Let's ask this question: If you had a reputation as being one of the most emotionally intelligent people in your personal and professional circles, how would that influence your habits and behavior from today onwards? How would it influence the way you manage stressful situations, difficult people, tough decisions, failure, change and uncertainty?

As you give this some thought, I invite you to take on this challenge. Think of yourself as "world class" when it comes to exercising your own emotional intelligence! View yourself as the Simone Biles or the Usain Bolt of your workplace! I guarantee it will alter the way you approach situations requiring emotional management and empathy, as well as how you navigate workplace complexities.

In watching my father's example through the years, it's clear to me that raising your level of emotional intelligence for professional growth not only makes good business sense, it is also a worthwhile endeavor because on a far more expansive scale, it makes you a better person to be around. And as it's been said time and again, *people like to do business with people they like.*

EI is a skillset we ought to embrace more fully, study more vigorously, and seek more aggressively, not just in our personal lives but in our professional lives as well.

Take the challenge. Be your own Bolt or Biles. Visualize yourself seeking—and *finding*—higher levels of emotional intelligence each and every day, **not** just because it leads us along a brighter professional path, **but** because it leads us along a better *life path* in general.

CHAPTER 6
Your Effect on Others Matters

"The effect you have on others is the most valuable currency there is."
–Jim Carrey

IN AN AGE OF DIGITAL distraction, where everything seems to command our attention at every moment, we're left with little room to stay focused in the present moment and little opportunity to really observe how we are moving through this world. This makes the task of being more mindful of our impact on others that much more challenging. It's a task that is easier said than done. Nevertheless, it is a task well worth doing.

Knowing what we know about the fact that the happiest people are those with meaningful and sustained connections, and knowing that happiness is something we all strive for, we miss out on the privilege of meaningful connections if we have no regard for our impact on others or how others experience us.

Writing this chapter coincided with a trip I recently made to Barcelona, Spain, to deliver a keynote presentation on the impact of emotional intelligence on customer experience. As I travelled this journey, I made the conscious decision to put away my digital gadgets and become keenly aware of everything and everyone around me. I wanted to observe and absorb as much as I could about my interactions with others and their interactions with me.

So on the flight to Barcelona, I paid close attention to the pilot, the flight attendants, the taxi driver who drove me to my hotel, the concierge who welcomed me so warmly to the hotel, the waitress who served me at the restaurant, the registration staff who greeted me at the conference, and all the people I met and interacted with at the conference.

The direct result of my enhanced awareness? I became supremely aware of the ways and the manner in which I influenced my interactions with others; an awareness that influenced—very positively, I might add—my thought patterns, my choice of words, and, indeed, my actions.

I noticed that the pilot spoke in a calm and reassuring manner when we hit some turbulence halfway through the flight, and it was this professional sensitivity on his part that allowed passengers to feel as comforted and unafraid, even in the midst of turbulence.

I noticed the awkward moments with my taxi driver, who *insisted* on speaking to me in Spanish, even though I told him with the few Spanish words I knew that I didn't really speak Spanish.

I noticed how polite, welcoming and engaging the hotel concierge was when I checked in.

All of my interactions along the way made me realize something vital and necessary: every encounter I had with others, no matter how brief or lengthy, produced an *emotional aftertaste:* that feeling inside that let me know whether I had just had a pleasant or unpleasant experience.

The fact of the matter is that we are constantly either receiving ourselves or giving to others this emotional aftertaste, and it's important to realize that this aftertaste—bad or good, positive or negative—carves an indelible impression into our own hearts and minds.

Whether we are aware of it or not, every interaction we have with others, be it with friends, family, co-workers or strangers, produces an effect—an *aftertaste*—and the good news is that we have the opportunity to play a significant role in determining whether these encounters leave a sweet or bitter aftertaste.

The power lies in the knowledge that the *choice* is ours.

To appreciate this, you only have to look to examples of interactions you've had with others that were either positively memorable or unfortunately regrettable. The reality is that we are constantly impacting others, whether consciously or unconsciously and, in both cases, that impact is often felt through our communication style and our actions towards others.

When it comes to our actions, here's an example of the conscious impact we can have: You see a homeless person begging on the street corner with a tattered cardboard sign in hand. All you have in your wallet are credit cards—no cash. It pains you to walk past without helping in some small way.

You remember that you still have an uneaten sandwich from the deli, and you offer that to them. They take it with gratitude and as you walk away, it brings a little smile to your face to know that you made some sort of difference; that you had a powerful, positive effect on someone else.

It is clear, in this case, that your actions produced a tangible and visible impact. At the heart of it, whether our conscious impact results in something positive or negative, it is visible to us, thus making us aware of how we're behaving.

The unconscious impact of our actions on others can be just as impressionable, in spite of the fact that we don't typically get to see the outcome in real time. While our unconscious impact can either be positive or negative, let's focus for a moment on the negative influences, simply because that is where there exists the greatest potential to cause harm.

Here's an example: You're going through some personal trials and tribulations in your life and talking to your close friends about it helps you feel better. This is especially true when you talk to the ones who always seem to be especially good at bringing you comfort with their gentle, non-judgmental words of wisdom.

On one particular day, after a two-hour conversation with a friend, she brings your attention to the fact that, while she enjoys helping you process through your issues, the conversation seems to always become a monologue, with you talking ninety percent of the time.

You find this disclosure a little shocking—perhaps even a bit hurtful—because none of your other friends have ever brought that to your attention. The truth of the matter is that the others were probably trying to be polite or didn't want to hurt your feelings; they didn't want to embarrass you by pointing out your proclivity for monopolizing the conversation.

A potential after-effect of behavior like this, if it goes unchecked, could result in your friends dreading to answer the phone when they see your name pop up on the screen.

When I reflect on my own situation, from the story I shared with you in the introduction, I clearly had an unconsciously negative impact on my dorm mates. While I wasn't *initially* aware of the impact of my behavior on them, the reality is that I still affected them negatively with actions that were emotionally bruising.

The sobering truth about unconsciously impacting others in a negative way is that if it's never brought to our attention, we continue unabated—and potentially suffer the consequences of social or professional isolation.

With respect to the impact we have when communicating, here's the bottom line: When it comes to how we communicate with others, it's important to remember that while we have access to all the words in the English language (or any other language) free of charge, if we don't use our words mindfully they can cost us a lot.

Think about a time you might have received critical feedback at work that was delivered in such a manner that it left you feeling emotionally battered. Or a time you might have made an honest mistake with a friend and found yourself on the receiving end of a harshly-worded e-mail that made you feel ashamed or embarrassed.

It's fair to say that almost none of us would voluntarily choose to spend our time around people who communicate with us in ways that make us feel miserable or leave us with a bad aftertaste. Much in the same way that we wouldn't condone this, it's important for us to check *ourselves* from time to time by asking ourselves questions that help us become more present and more mindful about the ways we choose to communicate with others.

One way to become more intentional in (and mindful of) your interaction with others, whether verbal or written, is to spend a few minutes beforehand reflecting on how you would want the other person to *feel* after their interaction with you.

I'm not insisting that you *control* how they will feel—you couldn't do that, anyway—I'm simply suggesting that it's a good thing to consider being more thoughtful and intentional with how you choose your words, ahead of time. This takes purposeful, mindful reflection and even thoughtful preparation.

If, for instance, you have to communicate with a lagging team member about picking up their pace in order to meet an important deadline, you would benefit from using language that, while serious in tone, still leaves them feeling positive and inspired to raise their level of performance.

Example: In one instance you could say something like, "You're currently the weak link in this project and it's causing us to fall behind with meeting our deadline." In another instance you could say something like, "While I know you have a lot on your plate, I would really appreciate you dedicating more time and attention to this important project to help the team meet this critical deadline."

The latter acknowledges them while gently encouraging them to change their behavior and, thus, improve their performance—but it *doesn't* leave them feeling wounded, which often results in them wasting precious time "licking their wounds" and soliciting sympathy from others. Equally important, the latter example shows what we've been discussing all along: empathy and emotional intelligence.

As another example, you might notice that your spouse has a habit of leaving drops of water around the bathroom sink (much to your annoyance). Here is one way you might address the issue: "Honey, I'm really tired of having to wipe up after you, because every time you brush your teeth, you splash so much water around unnecessarily and it makes a real mess."

This approach may very well put your spouse on the defensive and cause them to react in ways that unintentionally escalate the conversation in a negative direction. It might also cause resistance within them and keep them defiant just for the sake of it.

Alternatively, you could consider something like this: "Hey honey, I would be eternally grateful if you could help me out by taking a minute after you've brushed your teeth to wipe up the water that splashes around the sink."

Taking a few minutes to think about the impact of your words can make the difference between getting what you want and finding yourself in the middle of an unnecessary (and often protracted) battle.

When you think about everyday life scenarios, challenge yourself to think more deliberately about how you approach each and every one of your encounters. For example, when someone calls you and you don't recognize the number, is your immediate reaction to be rude and terse with them and even, sometimes, abruptly hang up the phone? When you're in a taxi and the driver inadvertently takes an incorrect turn, is your first instinct to yell in frustration and possibly berate them? When you're in your car and someone in front of you is driving slower than you think is appropriate, do you begin honking your horn incessantly?

Being more mindful of our impact on others is a daily and deliberate undertaking, with lots of moments when we have to catch ourselves spiraling down the wrong way and re-orient ourselves back to our better nature. Put simply, when it comes to our own behavior, we must monitor and self-correct constantly; it must become a pattern within us—almost an instinct.

Here are some guiding and self-reflective questions that can help you become more mindful of your impact on others on a daily basis.

When I interact with others, do they feel better or worse off because of my presence?

When someone says something that triggers me, do I immediately go on the offensive and attack them?

When communicating with someone else, how well do I listen to what they're actually saying, especially in moments when I disagree?

When I interact with others, do I monitor my body language to make sure I'm not giving off false or unintended signals?

When someone speaks to me, am I really present and listening or just waiting my turn to talk?

When I have a lot to say, do I monopolize the conversation or am I able to make room for others to share their opinions?

When I speak to others during a difficult conversation, am I aware of and in control of my tone of voice?

The most foundational of emotional intelligence skills is the one that calls on us to become more aware of ourselves and our own emotions. Keeping the above questions in mind as an occasional self-check will help you on your journey towards greater self-awareness. As you continue to grow your EI, you will indeed influence, with growing consistency, the emotional aftertaste you leave behind in positively memorable ways.

When I think about ways in which we can positively influence others, I'm reminded of a serendipitous moment that occurred just as I began writing this chapter.

It happened when I took a writing break to call an aunt to see how she was doing. I thought it would be an ordinary phone call much like all the others we usually have, centering around a few exchanged pleasantries and general inquiries about our immediate families.

As our conversation progressed, however, she shared a heartbreaking story of having just lost her best friend of fifty-three years. She lamented about how immensely her dear friend Evangeline had suffered before succumbing to pancreatic cancer, which had been misdiagnosed for an entire year. They had known each other since they were little girls in the fourth grade in Ghana, and her death had absolutely devastated my aunt.

Based on everything my aunt told me about the decades of both ordinary and extraordinary life experiences they shared together while travelling around the world, it sounded like Evangeline was an incredibly kind, fun-loving and generous human being. My aunt reflected on the fact that Evangeline always had a smile on her face and inspired the very best in others.

At her memorial service in London, my aunt told me that a number of people shared their personal testimony. It appeared that each person who spoke varied in age, from young millennials to a lady well into her eighties. It was extremely heartwarming for my aunt to see just how many people from different generations had been touched in one way or another by her best friend.

As we continued to chat, there was one thing she said that stood out to me. She said that listening to all the tributes that afternoon, you would have thought that everyone who spoke had first convened in a back room somewhere and coordinated what they were going to say about Evangeline.

It appeared that she impacted everyone in a similar way. According to my aunt, they all spoke of her "booming laugh" that was enough to lift up your spirits in moments you felt least like smiling. They shared stories that highlighted the warmth and strength of her hugs, and her attentiveness and empathy. When she spoke to you, it made you feel like you were the most important person in the room. It was unanimous: they all pointed out the fact that she always exuded an "air of peace."

Hearing this felt like an interesting coincidence to me. Just a few minutes earlier, I had been planning out what I was going to write in this chapter to support the idea that the effect you have on others matters, trying to figure out what real-life lessons I would use.

And now here was a real-life story right before me, reminding me that while people will experience each other differently, there ought to be a fundamental consistency with which we experience each other; a consistency in things like how we manage our emotions in challenging situations, how much integrity and honesty we show *even when no one is watching*, and how well we communicate with others in good times as well as bad times.

It was clear that Evangeline possessed a high level of self-awareness, self-mastery and empathy towards others and those who shared personal testimonials at her memorial service spoke of how these qualities manifested throughout her life, with consistency and uniformity. Put simply, emotional intelligence was woven into the fabric of her every move and her every thought, creating a beautiful tapestry of empathy, compassion and understanding. This is the very tapestry that we should —*all* of us—try mightily to duplicate.

After I hung up the phone, I began thinking more deeply about my own impact on others. It got me wondering how others experience me, in both my personal and professional circles, and whether there was a fundamental consistency in my overall treatment of others.

It also got me thinking about the fact that it's a real shame that, for the most part, we only receive these kinds of tributes when we're gone from this earth.

The truth of the matter is that we *all* want to be remembered favorably. We all hope that when we're gone, those who share their sentiments about who we were and how we lived can genuinely share them (and shine them) in a positive light. Ultimately, we want to be seen as having been a good friend, a good partner and a good colleague.

This revelation led me to a self-reflective question, which I invite you also to answer for yourself. *Am I currently living a life true to my values and in such a way that stays true to how I actually want to be remembered?*

While you ponder this question, here's another one to consider. If I picked out a handful of people in your personal and professional circles to pay tribute to you today, while you are still alive and kicking, what would they honestly say about you? I challenge you to summarize your thoughts below, being as true as you can to your current reality.

_____

_____

_____

While no one expects us to live our lives in perfect harmony with everyone around us, we ought to do what we can—whenever we can—to strive to be better in our thinking, our speaking, our *being.*

If you take a moment to really reflect upon what you just wrote down, are those words that you would be proud to hear? Is there room for you to grow into the kind of human being who is deserving of an amazing tribute?

I would like you to think for a moment about how you *actually* want to be remembered with respect to your impact on others around you. Jot this down in the space below. How do you want to be remembered?

_____

_____

_____

Now I would like you to look at these last two entries and personally assess whether there is a gap between what *is* and what you *want* there to be. If there is, what is *one thing* you can commit to that would help you bridge that gap?

_____

_____

_____

As you completed this exercise, you might have been one of the people who had this thought creep into your mind: "How others experience me is out of my control and not really my concern." While I agree that we cannot spend our days walking around worrying about what others think of us, I do believe that life is about relationships and because relationships are reciprocal, we have to care about our role in making them more meaningful.

Jim Carrey was right on the mark with his declaration that the effect we have on others is the most valuable currency there is. We all want to feel like we matter and feel that our presence makes some sort of difference. It's only fair that we acknowledge this desire in other people as well, and take purposeful steps to ensure that our presence manifests in productive and positive ways.

Caring about our impact on others is a vital ingredient in our personal and professional success. It ensures that we get to experience the kind of happiness that comes from having rich, meaningful and sustained connections with others. Caring about your effect on others is indeed a no-brainer, but it takes sustained effort and requires what I like to call *mindful intention*.

The daily work of becoming more aware of your thoughts and emotions and your behavior around others is essential in your journey toward emotional intelligence.

SECTION THREE

DARING TO CARE HAS ITS REWARDS

CHAPTER 7
Identifying and Maximizing the Emotional Benefits

*"Everything can be taken from a man but one thing: the
last of the human freedoms—to choose one's attitude in any
given set of circumstances, to choose one's own way."*
—Holocaust survivor Viktor Frankl

IN A NORMALLY FUNCTIONING SOCIETY, most of us are told to go to school, to work as hard as we can, and to remain focused along the way in order to achieve the best grades, the best job, and the best standard of living that we are capable of achieving. It has become the picture, the standard, and the very definition of success: If we do all of these things, take all of these necessary steps, strive constantly towards all of these pre-assigned and predetermined goals, our lives will be complete.

The emphasis, then, is placed on academic excellence and the resulting attainment of not just a decent, well-paying *job*, but a lucrative, long-lasting *career.*

What isn't given nearly enough focus and attention—and this is a mistake—is the need for us to invest in the kind of continuous emotional learning that deepens our human experience in a way that allows us to recognize, understand, and manage our own emotions to help us relate rightly to the world around us, to others, and ultimately, to ourselves.

Without having a pre-written Rule Book at our disposal about how we're supposed to go through life dealing with the things that challenge us on an emotional level, we are, for the most part, left to fend for ourselves, learning what we can—in bits and pieces—from our parents or from the wise and wonderful elders in our lives, or perhaps from popular self-help books, or, as is most often the case, by trial and error.

The good news is that you can commit to consciously working on your own emotional growth and maturity with deliberate practices that help you become more self-aware, self-mastered, and empathic. We examined some of these practices in the preceding chapters and now let's look ahead to some ways in which a greater level of emotional intelligence can benefit us.

While there are countless personal and professional benefits we gain from having a high EI, in this chapter we will focus on four in particular. More specifically, on the benefits of effectively managing our emotions, remaining flexible and resilient, managing stress and uncertainty, and positively influencing and motivating others. Let's take a deep dive:

The Benefit of Managing Emotions Effectively

On the most fundamental level, "managing your emotions effectively" simply means that when you feel an impulse or an external trigger, you don't react impulsively and without thought. *This is the essence of emotional mastery; the epitome of the definition of emotional intelligence*—the ability to tap into self-control strategies that guide how you react to anyone or anything at any given moment.

When I think about the benefits we gain from managing what we do with how we feel, I'm reminded of something that happened to me a few years ago that taught me an important lesson in emotional management.

It was a swelteringly hot and humid January afternoon in Accra, Ghana. My mother and uncle decided to treat me to one of my favorite restaurants at the Ghana Cocoa Board. Even though this was a rustic outdoor restaurant with sandy floors and beautiful, bright light, it was the *food* that was always a mouthwatering delight, and I quite enjoyed the rare occasion to sit under a magnificent mango tree to share lunch with two of my favorite people.

On this particular day, and in the sizzling heat, I made the irrational decision to wear the tightest jeans known to woman or man. We proceeded to our table, sat down, and ordered our food. A few minutes into waiting for our food to arrive, I felt something hit the top of my left canvas shoe. In an attempt not to bring attention to myself, I gently angled my head to the side and peeked under the table at my foot. I noticed a big, yellowing leaf a couple of inches from the top of my shoe and gently kicked it away in relief.

Our food arrived and I hungrily shoved heaping helpings of *Jollof Rice* (a popular dish) into my mouth, all the while ignoring the faint voice in the back of my mind that whispered, *Sylvia, you know that felt a little too heavy on your foot to have just been a leaf.*

After thirty minutes, my uncle paid the bill and we got up to walk back to his pickup truck. All of a sudden, I hunched over, dramatically cupping my hand against the inner side of my left knee. Something was in my jeans—moving around!—and I had the sinking feeling I knew what it was, even though I prayed that it was nothing more than a gentle grasshopper.

I looked at my uncle with fear in my eyes and desperation in my voice, and as calmly as I could, I said, "Uncle Harry, I need to get into your pickup truck right now to take my jeans off!" He looked at me as if I'd lost my precious mind.

The moment he realized I wasn't joking, he bolted to his truck, opening up the top flap and then the bottom flap so I could crawl in. I continued to cup my hand gently against the side of my knee to prevent whatever it was from running up any further. In the meantime, there were several strange men sitting at a nearby table, staring in amazement at my every move—and my mother, conveniently at a safe distance, freaking out and fearful of what her daughter would find.

How in the world am I going to get this thing out of my very tight, sweaty jeans—whatever this thing is—without ending up running around in my underwear or thrashing about wildly in the back of this truck? I thought to myself, trying desperately not to panic.

After a few hellraising minutes of trying to wedge the right pant leg off to give me enough material to wedge off the left, I finally got my jeans off. I bunched them up, slid open the side window of the pickup truck and threw my jeans at my uncle. He caught them, shook them out and there it was: A petrified silver-grey lizard about six inches long that dropped to the ground and went scurrying off to seek cover under the parked cars. (I realized, later, that the poor lizard was probably just as scared as I was!)

All along, and unbeknownst to me, it had been perched safely in the cool darkness of the bottom rim of my jeans … until I made a move to walk back to the truck. I was both horrified and relieved, because I am no fan of reptiles—and *certainly* not when that reptile is scurrying up my pant leg!

When all the commotion had died down, my mother walked back towards us sporting the kind of heartfelt, compassionate expression that any mother would have for a child in distress, and you know what she said to me?

"Sylvia, you need to start wearing more skirts and dresses. If you'd been wearing a skirt, this sort of thing would never have happened."

"Oh, Mama! Really?" I smirked with rolled eyes and an exasperated heart. (And for the record, I *still* haven't started wearing more skirts and dresses.)

When we later recalled the dramatic encounter with the lizard, my mother was deeply curious about how I managed to remain so calm in the restaurant. I told her that as much as I wanted to scream and pull my pants down immediately to free myself from the unknown invader, I knew I needed to focus on my *end goals*, which were to leave the restaurant intact and in pride, then get whatever it was out of my jeans safely without squashing it.

I also told her that as a professional speaker, I'm always looking for important lessons buried within everyday life events and believe it or not, as I was struggling to figure out how to get my jeans off, I kept whispering to myself, *There's a leadership lesson in this, I* know *there's a leadership lesson in this!* I realize, now, that this is what also helped me remain calm.

What I also came to realize was this: Every single one of us has "a lizard" in our lives. Those external people, places or things that can be thrust upon us unexpectedly, completely blindsiding us, and they have the potential to throw us completely off balance.

But instead of a *literal* lizard that scurries up your pants and causes all kinds of commotion, you might face, say, a "time management lizard"—as your boss abruptly changes an important deadline on you which throws you off completely, or a "family crisis lizard" that threatens to consume your time, cause great worry, and dissipates a tremendous amount of your emotional energy, or even a "health scare lizard" that keeps you in the doctor's office, or maybe even a "personal loss lizard" that breaks your heart and leaves you feeling empty, alone and disconnected.

By building up our emotional intelligence, however, we give ourselves the strength and the tools to conquer our "lizards" by enabling us to "grow the gap," as I like to call it. This means widening the gap between the time we feel triggered by something or someone and when we chose to do something about it. Think of it like a five-minute rule you might implement that says that you will always give yourself a space of five minutes between the time you receive a triggering e-mail and the time you actually reply to it.

When we manage our emotions effectively, we make fewer decisions that could result in regret. We also build the solid reputation of being level-headed and thoughtful, which goes a long way in determining how people in our personal and professional circles experience us.

I invite you to reflect on one way you could personally benefit from being in charge of your emotions during difficult, "lizard-inducing" times. Please jot down your thoughts in the space below:

_____

_____

_____

The Benefit of Managing Stress and Uncertainty

It's often said that "Change is the only constant in life"— which is indeed accurate. By its very nature, change brings with it a lot of uncertainty which can often lead us to feel more stress, strain and self-imposed anxiety than is necessary.

Having a healthy command over our emotions in the face of change allows us to remain even-tempered and to ride the waves of change and uncertainty as best as we can. So much of how we manage the potential stresses that come with being in unfamiliar territory depends on our self-talk and the way we choose to perceive what we're experiencing.

A couple of years ago, I delivered a ninety-minute emotional intelligence workshop to senior executives within a U.S. government agency. I deliberately waited until there were only fifteen minutes left in my presentation to call on two women sitting comfortably in the back row of a two-hundred seat auditorium. I politely asked them to gather all their belongings and transplant themselves all the way to the front of the room to sit in the two empty seats in the first row.

With a little hesitation and reluctance, they eventually moved to the front of the room. I'm sure you can imagine their body language as they dragged themselves from their comfortable, fairly secluded seats, not knowing what I was going to do next.

Once they sat down in the front row, I turned to one of them and asked if she wouldn't mind telling the rest of the group what she was thinking as she walked up to the front of the room. She chuckled and asked, "Do you *really* want to know?"

She continued, answering, "This is what I said: *Why is Sylvia pointing us out and asking us to get up from our chairs? I'm so comfortable where I am. I know my neighbors and we've gotten along very well. I don't know if she realizes that Happy Hour begins in thirty minutes! It doesn't make much sense to have to move now! Why is she putting us on the spot like this?*"

After I applauded them for moving to the vacant, front-row seats, I asked them each to reach under their chairs. What they did not realize, until then, was that I had taped an envelope to the bottom of each chair containing a one-hundred-dollar bill. This was their reward for being such good sports! Ironically enough, others in the room suddenly wanted me to select *them* to move seats! The reward became the incentive.

The point of my exercise with them was not to claim that at the end of every uncomfortable change there will be some sort of financial or material reward. No, the lesson was far more expansive than that. What I really wanted to highlight was the fact that oftentimes, when we're pulled outside our comfort zones, the first thing we relinquish is control over our self-talk. We begin to have, in some cases, "catastrophic" conversations with ourselves that spiral us out of control, magnifying and worsening what we're actually experiencing.

When we're faced with stressful and uncertain situations, our brain initially gives up control to the amygdala, the section of the brain which controls the way we react to an event that causes an emotion. It becomes really important for us to inject some logic and reasoning as well to help manage our self-talk. This is vital, because our self-talk often guides our thoughts and actions and we want to maintain as much control of our thoughts as we can.

Practicing the foundational emotional intelligence skill of self-awareness ensures that we orient our thoughts productively to help us manage the stresses of our lives. When we effectively manage stress and uncertainty, the benefits show up most explicitly in our overall good health, our uncluttered state of mind, and in our ability to maintain healthy, long-lasting personal and professional relationships.

Once again, I invite you to reflect on one way you could personally benefit from effectively managing stress and uncertainty in your life. Be as specific as possible:

_____

_____

_____

The Benefit of Flexibility and Resilience

An added benefit of being emotionally intelligent is that it empowers us with flexibility and resilience in trying times. It helps us adopt the kind of perspective that keeps our focus less on the thing that threatens to overwhelm us and more on what we can personally do to thrive in the face of it.

The tough reality is that we're living in a time of increasing global turmoil, unprecedented hardship and rising uncertainty— yet in spite of all this, *we must still find ways to persevere.* Working on your own self-awareness and emotional management builds you into a more resilient being.

At some point in our lives, we're all bound to face life situations and obstacles that will require us to be resilient in order to endure and triumph over them. Those life challenges could come in many forms, such as a health crisis that you're suddenly faced with, a financial challenge you can't seem to overcome, a toxic relationship that drains you of everything you've got, the sudden, heartbreaking loss of a loved one, and more. The possibilities and combinations are endless.

But with the help of emotional intelligence, we are able to choose a productive perspective to get us beyond the things that challenge us most. No one's story epitomizes this for me more than Veronique's. She was my father's former secretary and a dear family friend.

During the height of the genocide in Rwanda in 1994, an astonishing 800,000 people lost their lives in just one hundred days. On the 17th of March that year, Veronique was shot in the face at point blank range by a neighbor who on more than one occasion had dined in her home. He left her for dead and she was eventually rounded up by men conducting house-to-house searches. They carried her off to a mass grave.

Her daughter Francoise, with no idea of her mother's whereabouts, began searching the streets of the capital Kigali.

After countless hours of walking around desperately looking for her dear mother, her worst nightmare was realized when she spotted her mother lying in the midst of a pile of dead bodies.

When Francoise yelled for help, two good Samaritans came to her rescue. She hoped they would help transport her mother so she could give her a more dignified burial, but something miraculous happened.

As she gently pulled her mother's arm, she felt a very faint pulse. Even though her mother had a gaping hole in her face, with blood everywhere, *she was still alive*. The two men helped carry her mother one and a half miles up the dirt road to the nearest hospital.

After what felt like an eternity in emergency surgery, the doctor was able to save Veronique, in spite of all the blood she lost from the bullet shattering her eardrum, crushing her cheekbone and destroying her left eye.

Veronique's life had been spared once and was about to be spared a second time.

During the next night of her stay, rebels invaded the hospital. Armed with machetes, they killed everyone … almost. All the doctors, the nurses, and the patients were brutally massacred, save for a handful of people in a heavily guarded room that Veronique shared with a former army general because there were no other beds available when she was initially brought to the hospital.

After listening to her recount her ordeal, I noticed that she did so with such calmness and peace in her voice. I told her that I was in absolute awe of the fact that she seemed to harbor no anger or resentment towards the man who shot her and took so much away from her.

Veronique's response was priceless and positive: "I can focus on what I have lost and be bitter for the rest of my life, or I can focus on how blessed I am to have a second chance to live."

Her final words of wisdom that I will not soon forget were this: "I have come to learn that you must never allow someone who adds nothing to your life to control so much of it, and it is this realization that helps me keep everything in perspective."

While it's fair to say that most of us will hopefully never experience the heart-wrenching horror of genocide, we *will* all have our own trials and tribulations to overcome. With the help of our heightened emotional intelligence, we can indeed adopt the kind of perspective that allows us to see the greatest challenges of our lives in ways that prevent us from being broken by them.

EI allows us to navigate the most trying and testy circumstances in a way that helps us bounce back, because we focus less on what has or is happening to us and more on what we can do to endure it!

Please reflect on one way you could personally benefit from being flexible and resilient in the face of life's challenges and curve balls:

_____

_____

_____

The Benefit of Positively Influencing and Motivating Others

When we think about people with the greatest ability to positively influence and inspire others, among the many common traits they possess is a high level of emotional intelligence.

Being in tune with your own emotions and their impact on others, and having a sound, sustained ability to empathize with others, goes a long way in making you the kind of person who is truly inspiring and influential. Because emotionally intelligent people have a handle on their emotions even (perhaps especially) in the most challenging situations, they are still able to positively impact others, because of their ability to approach—and embrace—these situations in a level-headed manner.

We're living in a celebrity-driven culture where it often seems like it's the people with the brightest spotlight on them who have the greatest ability to influence and motivate others. While this is true in part, I believe that every day, in big and small ways, ordinary people are tapping into emotional intelligence to enable them to also have an important effect on others and inspire them in positive and productive ways.

Within the professional realm, having a heightened sense of self and social awareness can mean the difference between success and failure. If, for instance, you're in a leadership role of any kind, having a sound ability to influence and inspire others isn't just an advantage … it's a *necessity.*

In a sales situation for instance, your ability to positively influence others can be the difference between successfully overcoming buyer resistance and failing to make the sale. In an interview for a promotion or new job, for example, it could mean the difference between earning that well-deserved new position and letting it simply (and sadly) slip right through your fingers.

Once again, I invite you to reflect on one way you could personally benefit from being able to positively influence and motivate others:

_____

_____

_____

Knowing how to effectively manage your emotions and the stresses and uncertainties of life, while remaining flexible, empathetic, and resilient, will ensure that you're able to conquer whatever "lizards" crawl into your world—and trust me, they *will* crawl into your world, because this is life, after all.

Taking the time and making the sustained effort to invest in your journey of emotional growth and maturity has its emotional rewards, and these are rewards which will pay off not just today and tomorrow … but throughout the rest of your life!

CHAPTER 8
Touching (and Embracing) the Tangible Rewards

"It doesn't matter who you are, where you come from. The ability to triumph begins with you—always."
–Oprah Winfrey

NOTHING IS MORE GRATIFYING THAN the ability to integrate your emotional intelligence skills of self-awareness, self-mastery and empathy into a single, shining fabric that allows you to shine in both your personal and professional life.

In the previous chapter, we looked at some of the emotional rewards of a high EI. In this chapter, we'll focus on some additional rewards. We'll look at some of the tangible benefits such as enhanced clarity of thought, an increased ability to dispel and process stress, and the fundamental ability to not only survive but *thrive* in the face of crisis and/or potentially polarizing influences at home or in the workplace. In short, our ability to weave the threads of our own EI into the larger fabric of our daily lives is entirely possible—at work and at home as well. Let's start with clarity of mind:

The Tangible Benefit of Clarity of Mind

Amidst all the distractions, stressors (real and imagined) and negative influences constantly floating around us, maintaining a positive frame of mind can sometimes be a challenge. Sometimes we can get mentally bogged down by the burden of our own narratives, by the heft of our own personal and/or professional drama, and the weight of it only pulls us further away from the clarity of mind we seek.

A casual conversation I had with my dear friend Christie a few years ago brought this truth to light. It was a sunny, warm Friday afternoon in Washington, D.C., when I met Christie for coffee. She wanted my help figuring out a professional dilemma that she was facing.

She had been asked to speak at a women's conference to an audience of about two hundred women; Christie, I should add, is an extraordinary woman who has achieved amazing accomplishments, including record-setting distribution and extraordinary readership statistics for her women's journal.

But she was petrified at the thought of having to stand on stage and actually say something relevant and worthy of attention. Public speaking was just not one of her strengths. As she began sharing reasons why she was fearful about accepting the speaking invitation, it also became clear to me that she didn't feel she *deserved* to be there.

As we talked more, I began to appreciate the depth of her deeply set hesitation. Christie's native language is Spanish, and even though she spent most of the past four decades of her life in the United States speaking English, she was frequently teased about her accent, her grammar and the general way she spoke. She told me that even to this day, people still tease her about the grammar in her text messages. All of this insecurity and doubt clearly compromised her perception of herself and dramatically undermined her self-confidence—a real shame, given that Christie is one of the brightest people I know.

Christie also told me that this lifelong torment became the main reason she didn't teach her only child Spanish. She didn't want her to have to endure all the tortuous teasing and bullying she endured through the years for not speaking the "Queen's English."

As she continued to lament her situation, I assured her that I understood how she felt, but that I still wasn't buying any of what she was saying about being unworthy of the opportunity that lay before her. You see, I had worked with Christie in the past, at a time when she was triumphantly fighting a very courageous battle with breast cancer. I knew just how talented she was and just how hard she worked at everything she did, in spite of what she faced. So, I just wasn't buying it.

At one point in our conversation, I looked her squarely in the eyes and gently said, "Christie, that's an expensive story."

With some confusion on her face, she asked me what I meant. The way I saw it, I explained, the idea of "not being good enough because of imperfect English," had become the sole narrative … and that narrative was holding her back; constricting her growth.

It was this same narrative that robbed her of the opportunity to teach her now eighteen-year old daughter her precious Mother language. It was this same narrative that caused her to endure four, agonizing years mustering the courage to do her very first real estate listing presentation, and it was this same narrative that was about to cost her the opportunity of a lifetime—to stand before an audience of eager, well-respected women craving to learn best practices from her shared stories of strength, professional acumen, and history-making accomplishments.

The reason I called it an *expensive* story is because as Christie looked back at everything it had cost her to hold onto her own, destructive narrative, it slowly began to dawn on her how expensive it had all become. She stepped up to my challenge, however, and made the purposeful effort to replace her destructive narrative with something far more appealing, like, "I will no longer let the way I speak get in the way of my destiny. I was chosen for this role because they value me and I absolutely *deserve* to be on that stage."

I'm happy to report that Christie accepted the speaking invitation and received a standing ovation at the end of her presentation.

Speaking with her in the coffee shop that day made me realize that we all have a "story" and the saddest part about our *expensive* stories is that, for the most part, they aren't even *accurate*. Yet still, they have an inordinate amount of buying power— of *staying* power—which is unfortunate because our personal narratives dictate so much of who we become and what we do in life.

Expensive stories are chronically disempowering because they often dictate our actions (or inactions) with undesirable consequences. One of the most effective methods to overcome these destructive narratives is to make more of a concerted effort to expand our own self-awareness, thus deepening our clarity of thought. Exploring this layer within ourselves— the ability to stop the destructive narrative and replace it with something far more empowering and inspiring—will keep us headed in a positive and productive direction.

I invite you to reflect on some of your own narratives and think about one that might not be serving you well. Briefly jot down what that "story" currently is. Also examine what it's costing you to continue to hold on to it. Lastly, consider creating a *different* story, a more empowering story that can help propel you forward.

Your Expensive Story	The Cost	Your New Story

The Tangible Benefit of Reduced
Pressure and Stress from Conflict

Most of us live in increasingly diverse societies where we interact with people from varying backgrounds, viewpoints and approaches to life. While these differences ought to be celebrated for the richness they can add to our own lives, they are sometimes the very things that can become our greatest sources of conflict. It is our ability to master our EI that will determine how successful we are at interacting and communicating with our own richly diverse surroundings.

We don't have to look very far to get a sense of just how much our differences are creating dangerously toxic conflicts. What is important to remember, here, is that *conflict in and of itself is not inherently bad or good.* It is simply an indication that our opinions or perspectives differ from those with whom we are interacting.

Put plainly, conflicts arise because of differences of approach, opinion and method, and since none of us are exactly alike, we're bound to encounter conflicts throughout our personal and professional lives. In spite of this reality, I believe that our world is far better served by the richness and diversity of our collective selves than it would be if we were all exactly the same. Conflict is sometimes the price we have to pay. Conflict, indeed, can have a very positive outcome … as long as we identify and utilize the tools we need to control our reaction to this conflict.

At home, for example, conflicts might arise if you and your spouse/partner have fundamental differences in your child-rearing principles and practices. While one of you might believe that corporal punishment is an acceptable form of discipline, the other might prefer to simply have a healthy, heartfelt conversation with the kids, allowing them to reflect on their bad behavior.

Stresses and pressures from conflict in the home could also arise from differing approaches to potentially dicey issues like household cleanliness, with one person being a little too *carefree* and the other being a little too obsessive-compulsive about how clean the house ought to be at all times.

In the workplace, for instance, you might run into conflicts with a co-worker over issues that point towards incompatible interests, undesirable office politics, personality clashes, dramatically different workplace habits, or even conflicts over gender identification or cultural diversity. The list of potential conflict in the workplace is seemingly endless.

How we each handle ourselves within conflict situations is what makes the difference between resolving things productively and escalating the conflict to undesirable and unproductive levels.

While we often think of "conflict management" as something that we focus upon only during tense situations or actual moments of conflict, it's what emotionally intelligent people do before a conflict even arises that is worth noting. How does someone with high emotional intelligence move about successfully and efficiently in both the office and the home? By using their effective skills of self-awareness and self-mastery to ensure that they remain vitally aware of how they are feeling and the impact those feelings and emotions can have on others. This self-awareness, in turn, greatly reduces the chances of conflict.

People with a high EI also develop a habit of tactfully helping others through stressful and emotional situations. They do this by taking time to empathize with others, seeking to understand different perspectives and they adjust (or expand) their own perspectives to consider alternatives.

Some of the other reasons why emotionally intelligent people reap the benefits of good conflict management is because they are able to do the following:

1. Frame issues productively,

2. Avoid personalizing situations, and,

3. Use reflective listening to their strategic advantage.

Let's break it down:

They Frame Issues Productively

When we find productive ways to react to and control (to the extent that we can) our external circumstances and encounters, it can have a dramatic effect on our attitude, thoughts and actions. It essentially helps us widen our perspective and deepen our understanding and appreciation of this complex world around us.

If, for example, as a project manager, you're a stickler for punctuality and efficiency, and someone walks into your meetings continually late or unprepared, such behavior could easily become a negative trigger and a potential source of conflict.

While you might *feel like* sending out a punitive or angry-sounding email to the late-comer, or issue threats of what will happen in the future if their tardiness continues, your actual *behavior* could be a completely different manifestation: You could gently remind them of how critical it is that they show up on time, plus, you could also try to get to the bottom of their lateness. Perhaps it's because they were genuinely tied up in another meeting? Or could it be that they don't feel that their contributions are valued within meeting discussions? Might there be another, more compelling reason of which you are simply not aware? The employee or manager with the higher EI will be able to master his or her emotions and even look beyond the current situation in an effort to resolve the potential conflict. This is EI at its finest.

But let's get back to the example of how best to handle the perpetually tardy employee by employing our emotional intelligence: Consider reframing the situation so that you do not see it as a personal affront or a blatant form of disrespect, but rather as an opportunity to improve some aspect of your meetings to inspire more participation and ownership from team members.

They Avoid Personalizing Situations

So often conflict situations escalate during moments when we take things too personally. When this happens, our ego and our insecurities get in the way and obstruct our ability to react and behave in an emotionally intelligent manner.

Emotionally intelligent people are able to set their ego aside and ask themselves clarifying questions that greatly reduce the chance of them becoming personally (and unnecessarily) offended. Questions like, "Is it possible they didn't mean to disrespect me? Could I possibly have been clearer in making my request?"

All of these scenarios are worthy of consideration.

They Use Reflective Listening to their Strategic Advantage

When we are triggered by something someone has said or done, we lose our capacity to *really* listen. In those moments, without even realizing it, we take what ought to be crucial listening time and use it instead to preoccupy ourselves with how we're going to respond. In short, we skip ahead in an effort to formulate a response without actively, mindfully absorbing what is actually being communicated.

Because emotionally intelligent people typically have a good handle on their emotional triggers, they are able to effectively focus their attention on the other person and listen with mindful intention. They are grounded in the knowledge that their role in any conversation is to add value—which cannot happen if their emotions get the best of them and place them on the offensive.

That added value you bring could simply come in the form of allowing the other person the chance to feel heard and validated. So much of the tension we feel during a conflict situation arises when we feel we are not being heard.

While it might sometimes feel like an unnecessary expense of mental and emotional energy, it's amazing what can be accomplished when the ego is tamed. Active, reflective listening facilitates a deeper understanding of the other person's position, allowing you to ask penetrating, thoughtful questions at the same time.

The Benefit of Increased Productivity
in the Face of Change

There's a common belief that the fear of change is high on the list of things that most people fear. The way I see it, we don't really fear change itself as much as we fear what we think we will lose in the process of enduring the change. If you think about it, we experience change all the time, which isn't always a bad thing.

We change the places we eat, the destinations to which we travel, the people we date or marry, the cars we drive, the places we live, the places we work, the friendships we make, and so much more. Here's the bottom line: When we *perceive* that the change we're about to experience will produce negative or destructive results, we resist it.

Similarly, when we *perceive* the upcoming change will yield positive, productive results, we embrace it. As human beings, our mere perception of a situation strongly influences the manner in which we respond to that situation. Very much like a game of smoke-and-mirrors, our ultimate goal should be to keep our attention trained on the image itself—rather than our *perception* of the image.

I witnessed this first-hand through separate conversations I had with two friends a few years ago. Both Damian and Sarah were facing jobs they hated, and it became necessary for both of them to evaluate whether it was time to make a move into the unknown to find another place of work.

Sarah had complained to me for years about just how much she disliked her job and it puzzled me to think of why she wouldn't make the move to find another job after so many years of being unhappy there. I tried in vain on a few occasions to help her find the courage to make the move, but I was unsuccessful in my attempts.

Sarah was a very hard-working and dedicated employee, but sadly, her contributions at work were grossly undervalued and underappreciated. Her fear of the unknown and her anxiety about the possibility of a new position prevented her from making a move; of taking a leap of faith.

Damian, on the other hand, approached things a little differently. While he also complained about his job and about how miserable his boss was making everyone, he became actively focused on finding a new job because he finally realized that life was too short to spend another minute in misery.

So what did he do? He sought assistance with reviewing and updating his resume and cover letter, and became far more strategic and methodical about applying for jobs.

As a direct result of his efforts, Damian landed a position three weeks after he began his search! And based on the reviews he read online from current and past employees about his prospective company, he felt comfortable enough to accept the job offer. I commended him for his diligence, his pro-active approach, and his ability to make a major decision based on *facts*, rather than on fear.

In contrast, Sarah seemed to find every excuse known to man as to why it was difficult to leave her current job and find a new one—and as a result, her dissatisfaction deepened, which also became burdensome to her closest friends because they got to hear about it more often than they would have cared to.

I can report that as of this writing, Damian is still in his new position, where he tells me that he feels valued and relevant, and he is happy to have a manager who relates to the staff like human beings. Sadly, Sarah remains stuck in her old position, though she's made a promise to herself to make a move soon.

Sarah's and Damian's situations highlight an essential truth: Familiarity is easy and change is difficult. Even when we're dissatisfied or deeply uncomfortable with the status quo, as in Sarah's case, it often feels easier and safer to stay with the familiar than venture off into the unknown.

As renowned author and speaker Robin Sharma once put it, "The seduction of safety is always more dangerous than the illusion of uncertainty." The good news is that because so much about change has to do with how we perceive it, we have the power to change our own perceptions and thus influence how we handle change.

Emotionally intelligent people consciously choose to view change through a productive lens, asking themselves "Gateway" questions that help them focus on the possibilities and not the potential losses.

They ask questions like, "What is this change present in my life to teach me, and how can I learn from it? What is a potentially positive outcome that can result because of this change?" These are all questions that focus the mind in a positive, forward-moving direction.

One of the most important parts of navigating change productively has to do with our "self-talk." When faced with change and uncertainty, one of the first things that deteriorates are the conversations we have in our own heads about what is unfolding before us. This, in turn, affects our attitude, our mood and ultimately the decisions we make.

The self-awareness that comes from being emotionally intelligent keeps us mindful of our self-talk to ensure that we have empowering conversations with ourselves during challenging or turbulent times, rather than demoralizing, destructive conversations.

The Tangible Benefit of Overall Leadership Effectiveness

What is the first thing that comes to mind when you think of what makes someone an effective leader? Or perhaps ask yourself these questions: Who is the best leader you've ever worked with? And what exactly was it about their leadership style that made them a great leader?

I venture to say that beyond the tangible and practical things they did (or do) to efficiently execute their leadership skills, so much of why you look up to them is because of *how they make you feel.* I believe that the most effective leaders do what they can to positively influence the emotional aftertaste of their leadership and this is the reason we don't ever forget their impact on us.

In answering this question for myself, a former senior manager came to mind. I worked with Gina at a leading global accounting and consulting firm. Aside from being a brilliant Change Management Strategist whose expertise put her head and shoulders above everyone else in our male-dominated office environment, she had an amazing ability to manage her emotions in the most challenging of times.

Unlike other managers in the office who typically took out their anger and frustration on their staff, Gina was always very levelheaded. She was also very mindful of her impact on people around her, and as a result of this mindfulness, she checked in often with her staff to gauge how they were feeling about various aspects of their work.

Gina made a conscious effort to articulate how much she valued the individual and collective contributions of everyone on her team, and her deep satisfaction was reflected in her infectious smile and overall warm, inviting energy. There are leaders out there who try to mask their own insecurities by resorting to management methods based on fear and intimidation, but the most effective leaders understand that legendary leadership must begin with *self-leadership*. It must start on the inside then, and work its way out. As Dee Hock, founder of Visa, once said, "If you want to lead, invest at least forty percent of your time in leading yourself."

Most of us know what it feels like to be led by someone who is even-tempered, assertive yet thoughtful and mindful of how they communicate and make others feel. Sadly, many of us also know what it feels like to be led by just the opposite.

If you are privileged to play a leadership role in your professional life, I invite you to reflect on how you can leverage emotional intelligence skills to enhance your own leadership effectiveness and ability to positively influence others.

It is clear that investing time and energy into growing our emotional intelligence has countless rewards. Nothing feels as good as being able to wake up each day with clarity of mind, ready to live productively in our personal and professional lives, in spite of the challenges that we face on a daily basis.

These are all important goals. And with hard work, enhanced focus, and a genuine desire to learn from the lessons we've examined thus far, you, too, can achieve these goals.

CHAPTER 9
The Courage that Comes from Clarity

*"There are few things more powerful than a
life lived with passionate clarity."*
— Erwin McManus

ONE MORNING MORE THAN A decade ago, in the middle of taking a shower, I had an epiphany. I don't know about you, but I feel like some of my deepest thinking happens in the shower, right alongside my "legendary" singing, but, well, we'll leave that tender topic for another book. For three years leading up to that moment, I had been working very hard in my role as a Regional Director, successfully meeting and exceeding rigorous educational sales goals.

That morning in the shower, as I reflected on the past few years, I finally realized just how mentally and emotionally exhausted I had become. In that moment, I knew I needed to make a major shift in my life. Something had to give. I had been running on auto-pilot, in a highly demanding role managing teams of people, and we chased ambitious new sales targets week in and week out.

The constant travel, crisscrossing all over the country just about every week, had also taken its toll. The number of friends' weddings, baby showers and significant life events that I'd missed were too numerous to count. And to top it all off, I had to work under a manager whose leadership style lacked empathy and often left me emotionally drained.

All of the stress and pressure had begun to affect my health and I knew, deep down in my heart, that I couldn't continue that way any longer. To everyone on the outside, my life seemed in perfect harmony—but on the inside, I was struggling with a work experience that had become soul-sucking.

I made a decision that morning to leave my job, and I promptly followed up on that decision by giving my employer five weeks' notice. This wasn't an easy decision to make because we were in the throes of an economic recession and I was about to walk away from a steady, lucrative income that was three times more than anything I'd ever earned in my life. But once I faced the decision with courage and clarity, I realized that my mental and emotional health had to take priority over any pursuit of financial wealth.

For years later—from that pivotal moment to this very day—I've been struck by the vital role that EI plays in helping us gain the clarity we need to become more emotionally courageous. The role it plays in equipping us with the necessary self-awareness and mastery over our emotions that is imperative to us facing and overcoming life's discomforts and difficulties with greater ease. (Also, on a side note, I used the words "emotional courage" deliberately, because I believe that all courage is emotional. If courage, as Google defines it, is "the ability to do something that frightens us and have strength in the face of pain and grief," it doesn't get more emotional than that.)

As I thought more about the relationship between courage and clarity, I became increasingly interested in wanting to hear the perspectives of ordinary people, so, I posed a question to numerous friends and colleagues and this was what I asked them:

Think of a personally challenging situation you previously experienced, maybe a toxic relationship, difficult work environment, personal loss or facing failure—whatever the situation, make it yours. Think about how you handled that situation when it occurred. With the benefit of hindsight and greater clarity, do you think you'd have the courage *to handle the situation differently if you were facing it today?*

Before I share some of the feedback I received, I want us to travel back to that fateful day which I described at the very beginning of the book, when I lost my temper (and perhaps, momentarily, even my mind) and threw chairs across the restaurant dining room.

At the time, I had allowed an unbelievable amount of pent-up frustration and anger to boil and bubble inside of me. I didn't have the courage to confront the situation in a way that would have soothed my sanity and enhanced my overall work experience.

Years later, and with the benefit of hindsight and clarity, I *certainly* would have handled the situation differently: I would have approached the general manager calmly and professionally to express how I felt about the toxic work environment that had been created. This might at least have given him an opportunity to address my concerns in a rational manner, rather than having to face the fury of my meltdown.

As you read through the excerpts below, I invite you to think about your own experiences. What newfound clarity, insight, and wisdom have given you a different perspective?

Excerpt 1

Situation:

"I was in toxic relationship with someone who brought out some of the worst parts of my personality. In many respects, the disrespect I showed mirrored the fear I had in trying to succumb to societal expectations."

Clarity and Hindsight:

"With the benefit of clarity and wisdom, today I would have the courage to realize that my irrational behavior reflected my fear of losing a dream that I thought I always wanted and needed to have a satisfying life. Today I would have the courage to recognize that dreams can and sometimes need to change, so why not change them? No sense in ruining lives over some dreams. Today, I constantly tell myself that there's no award in heaven for stubbornness."

Excerpt 2

Situation:

"In the early 2000s, I bought a relatively large five-bedroom home for my wife and I and our two small children. Trying to maintain so much house put a heavy strain on my finances and my mental state. Three years later, the housing market crashed and we lost half the value of our home. Five years

after that, I had to short-sell the house with an out-of-pocket expense in the tens of thousands of dollars."

Clarity and Hindsight:

"I reflect on the fact that just because all my peers were buying big homes, I didn't have to do the same thing to feel validation. Today, with more clarity and wisdom, I now live in a humbler, cozier place and I don't mind having my fancy friends over because I know who I am and that is separate and apart from what I have."

Excerpt 3

Situation:

"In my 20s, I was a volunteer rape counselor. I would show up with my ten-pound binder and answer all the victims' questions before they had to endure all kinds of swabs, pokes and prods. One unforgettable day, in an effort to comfort a girl who had just been sexually assaulted in an alley, I put my foot in my mouth by inadvertently minimizing her experience by saying that at least it wasn't a vaginal rape. As the words left my mouth, I knew what I just said was absolutely horrible and there was nothing I could do to take it back. Horrified, I apologized profusely and did my very best to comfort her, but I knew the damage was done."

Clarity and Hindsight:

"I no longer force myself just to say something to lessen someone's pain or suffering. So often I found myself needing to say, 'Well, at least....' in an effort to make someone feel better or try to get them to realize that it wasn't as bad as it could have been. With clarity and wisdom, I would have said, 'What

has happened is horrific and there is absolutely no excuse for it, but you will get through this. It will take time, but you will cross from victim to survivor.'"

Excerpt 4

Situation:

"On only my second shift working in my very first restaurant job in Los Angeles, one of the managers came up to me at the host stand and grabbed my behind in such a bold and aggressive manner. After standing there in complete shock at what just happened, I burst into tears when the senior manager came to ask me what was wrong. I couldn't talk and instead I walked out and quit that day."

Clarity and Hindsight:

"Looking back, I regret not speaking out against him that day. I would have spoken up and expressed my feelings instead of ignoring them. With more clarity, I would have the courage to stand up for what I believe in and trust myself and my thoughts."

Each of these scenarios show us one thing: That challenging life situations happen to all of us. While we might not always react the way we would have liked, every trial or tribulation presents us with an opportunity for personal growth. As Dr. Maya Angelou often said, "When you know better, you can do better."

While we cannot erase the past circumstances or roll back the hands of time to create "do-over" situations, the good news is that we *can* tap into the deep well of our emotional intelligence to ensure that we embrace those challenges and difficulties in more empowering ways. The wonderful thing about EI is that it helps us to not have to depend on the benefit of hindsight in order to be our best selves each day. As we grow our self-awareness, we make better decisions in the present moment.

How you see emotional courage can look very different from how others see it. You might, for instance, see it as being true to yourself no matter what others think, or making a difficult decision when neither option is an easy choice. Others might see emotional courage as not judging themselves in a situation they normally would or letting their guard down in places where they don't need to have it up.

The one thing I think we can all agree on is that there are countless ways we benefit, grow and mature from exercising our emotional courage. Let's take a deeper look at two ways in particular.

Freedom to Have Difficult Conversations

For most of us, being put in a situation where we have to have a difficult conversation isn't something we relish. Difficult encounters and challenging conversations feel caustic and angst-ridden. This is because most of the time, those conversations revolve around us having to discuss a delicate subject or deliver unpleasant news or address an issue or behavior that needs to change.

The mere *thought* of having these kinds of conversations can stir up anxiety, fill us with trepidation and consume our minds in very distracting ways. At the heart of it, difficult conversations make most of us uncomfortable and if we had a choice, we'd opt to avoid having them altogether. The only problem is that putting off having the conversation doesn't make the need to have it go away. And the longer the conversation is delayed, the more deeply entrenched the situation becomes.

Case in point: I recently had to practice what I preached when faced with the uncomfortable situation of having to ask my lovely neighbors (and I mean that), to either not play their musical instruments at night or sound-proof their newly constructed basement music studio.

Twice a week, until quite late in the evening, they invited friends over for some sort of band practice or jam session, and unfortunately, the sound of drumming, strumming and singing easily penetrated my walls. For a few months, I mulled over how I would address this issue, not wanting to hurt their feelings or make myself feel guilty for suggesting that they address the problem.

What I had to remind myself, however, was the fact that if I approached them calmly, gently and with mindful intention, I stood a very good chance of achieving the desired results. When addressing them, it was also important for me to avoid using the word "but," which I believe is a word that can sabotage our best intentions by negating our honest attempt to convey empathy, compassion and sincerity.

In a nutshell, this is what I said:

"I know how much you enjoy your new studio and (*I was tempted to use "but" here*) I would like your help in figuring out a solution to the sounds that travel through my walls. Unfortunately, it is pretty distracting and I want to find a solution that can keep us both happy."

They ultimately opted to sound-proof their basement because they had the means, which ensured that they could continue to enjoy their jam sessions well into the night ... or whenever they wanted.

Sometimes the emotional courage we develop in order to have difficult conversations can come from our gaining clarity about how, precisely, we plan to address our concerns. In other words, being deliberate about (and mindful of) our choice of words even before we speak is extremely helpful. I'm not saying that every time you approach a difficult conversation, you will have full control over the outcome simply by your choice of words. I do believe however, that thinking positively about how you're going to approach the conversation *before the conversation occurs* is part of what arms us with the emotional courage we need.

I realize that it's often easier for us to have difficult conversations with people we perceive as unpleasant or unpalatable. Perhaps in those instances, it's because we perceive them in a negative light and are therefore less inclined to care about how we would make them feel. My neighbors, for example, are truly nice people—which made it more challenging for me to muster the courage to confront them in the first place.

Emotional courage allows us to see our vulnerability not as a weakness, but rather as a strength. If you have a tough conversation looming on the horizon, I encourage you to think more deliberately, *ahead* of time, about how best you can frame the conversation to ensure that your words are compassionate, caring and thoughtful.

Let's examine the next benefit of emotional courage, and perhaps you will better understand my advice about word choice.

Ability to Set Aside Our Ego

When we combine aspects of our personality with our talents and our abilities, we get the foundation of what we call our ego. Oftentimes, this identity which is of our own making, is a dynamic and ever-changing part of our personality and it can play an instrumental role in creating emotional drama in our lives.

The very essence of emotional courage is having the ability to put our ego aside even in the face of challenging, threatening or uncomfortable situations. In my previous example about my neighbor and their loud music, if your first thought was, *why should I have to choose my words mindfully when they're being so inconsiderate by playing loud music during week nights*?

Then I would argue that, while you are justified in feeling that way, your ego is probably the "voice" that is speaking the loudest. It is our ego that often has us seeing vulnerability as weakness, and if we respond to being prodded by our ego, we end up in unnecessary conflict situations because our ego refuses to "succumb" to using more empathy and compassion when handling potentially testy situations.

When you exercise emotional courage, your ego gets pushed out, which can make for a difficult internal battle. It's important to recognize when your ego is trying to lead you, so that you can set it aside to help ensure the best possible outcome as you deal with situations that might feel threatening to your beliefs, values, or habits.

The reality is that we are never going to *completely* get rid of our ego or totally silence its presence in our lives. What we therefore have to do is focus on chipping away at the often-inaccurate beliefs that make up our ego. We can do this by remaining conscious of our self-talk and challenge ourselves when we think our ego is trying to take over. Our self-awareness and mastery over our emotions can also help keep our ego at bay.

When we set aside our ego, it gives us the courage to embrace feedback and criticism productively, accept blame when we're wrong, abandon the personal narratives that no longer serve us, remain true to our core values—even when inconvenient—and allow others to see us even when we're not at our best selves.

As you can see, there is indeed a lot we can gain by exercising emotional courage, but in order to fully realize these benefits we must first do the hard, sometimes messy yet important work of gaining clarity about who we are, how we feel, and how we manage what we feel.

The truth of the matter is that on our meandering journey through life, we will never arrive at a destination called Final Self-Awareness or Final Self-Mastery. Pursuing these vital emotional intelligence skills is a never-ending, life-long journey that promises one thing:

That if we stay the course, if we work at this daily and diligently, we will eventually develop the emotional courage needed to reap the riches of a more satisfying, meaningful and rewarding life.

That courage we seek doesn't happen without greater self-knowledge and we cannot know ourselves better if we don't uncover our blind spots, move past our egos and manage our emotions effectively. Let's look at these more closely.

Exposing Blind Spots and Taming Our Ego

You've probably heard the saying that *you cannot change what you do not acknowledge*. Well, when it comes to our blind spots, as defined by Merriam Webster's dictionary as, "a tendency to ignore something especially because it is difficult or unpleasant," we need trusted friends and colleagues to help us see what we don't see.

Why should you care about discovering aspects of who you are that you can't even see, especially if it makes you uncomfortable? The short answer is this: *Because your personal and professional growth depends on it.* Knowing your blind spots is a big step towards developing greater self-awareness, which directly contributes to us having more personal courage.

As you expose your blind spots, you might discover a behavior or experience that occurs repeatedly which could be interfering with your productivity at work, or your health, or some aspect of your relationship with others. Perhaps your blind spot could be that you're someone who values being right more than anything else, or you get caught up saying "yes" when you'd rather say "no," or you don't defend yourself in difficult conversations because you hate conflict, or you're settling for less than you really want in life because you don't feel worthy or deserving.

What we ought to realize most is that our ego is what gets in the way of these crucial self-discoveries, and we have to remind ourselves that like every other human being, we are a work in progress and that it's okay to *not* be perfect, because no one else is, nor will they ever be.

We cannot live in greater alignment with who we were meant to be and live our best lives if we don't confront the parts of ourselves that could be holding us back. The bottom line is that the more we know *all* aspects of ourselves, the more courage and self-belief we have.

Embracing and Managing All of Our Emotions Productively

Each of us has a front row seat to what I call the "Me Observatory"—that vantage point from which we get to observe our emotional reactions to the things that happen to us. It's challenging to observe yourself from this viewpoint because this up-close-and-personal perspective inevitably introduces us to some vulnerabilities that emerge from confronting difficult emotions like sadness, fear and anger.

It doesn't help that most of us live in cultures that encourage and celebrate the outward expression of emotions deemed positive, while frowning upon and even outright rejecting emotions deemed to be negative. If you're alive and breathing, you're bound to experience emotions that will test you from time to time. It's important to realize just how okay it is to sometimes not feel okay when juggling these tough emotions.

When we feel sadness, for example, we often expend so much emotional energy fighting to feel anything but what we are actually feeling. We fall into the seduction of thinking that we are supposed to feel happy and peachy all the time and we judge difficult emotions as something to be escaped from rather than experienced.

This internal fight only serves to cloud our thinking and rob us of the courage we need to fully embrace *all* of our emotions as part of the human experience of being alive. When you're dealing with something emotionally difficult, there is nothing more generous you can do for yourself than to be kind to yourself.

As you reflect upon your own life situations, think about where in your life you could practice more emotional courage. The road to knowing and understanding ourselves better is paved with occasional bumps of discomfort, but as award-winning psychologist Dr. Susan David reminds us, "Discomfort is the price of admission to a meaningful life." We inject more meaning into our lives each time we are courageous enough to stand tall in our moments of difficulty or discomfort.

It is these moments—facing them, rather than fearing them; embracing them rather than escaping them—that truly define the price of admission to a meaningful life.

And this is a price we should *want* to pay!

CHAPTER 10
Let the Journey Begin!

"We delight in the beauty of the butterfly, but
rarely admit the changes it has gone
through to achieve that beauty."
−Dr. Maya Angelou

MOST OF US HAVE HEARD the old adage attributed to Chinese philosopher Lao-Tzu, reminding us that, "A journey of a thousand miles begins with one step." When it comes to the never-ending journey of growing our emotional intelligence, this is no exception. It's the small steps we take to become more self-aware, to better manage our emotions and their impact on others that makes a mighty difference.

If we look back to the days of our very early youth, when we were barely old enough to take our first steps, most of us had already begun receiving messages, expectations, and words of wisdom from our parents, loved ones and even well-meaning strangers.

These were messages—life lessons, really, shared with love and intention—about being kind, about being generous, about being thoughtful and empathetic. While these are basic values that most of us still hold dear, the fact of the matter is that we don't always live them out as deliberately as we should. We fall short.

Yes, we certainly become very deliberate in our intentions when those intentions concern our lives and livelihood. We are deliberate, for example, about where we want to live, deliberate in our search for the most rewarding career path and the more suitable life partner, even deliberate in planning our next vacation and the acquisition of our next new automobile. But when it comes to showing that same amount of care and deliberation about embracing healthy habits that make us more aware of our own emotions and the impact that those emotions have on others around us, we often fall short.

Midway through this book, I issued a challenge that, if fully embraced, has the potential to inspire a beautiful new way of being and a beautiful new way of thinking. I want to circle back to that challenge here, in this final chapter, in hopes that you have fully absorbed the immense value of building a reputation as an emotionally intelligent being.

Usain Bolt and Simone Biles, in their quest to be the best possible versions of themselves as world-class athletes, embraced the habits and behaviors needed to propel them to greatness. Following that same, purposeful pattern, you, too, can tap into your own emotionally intelligent habits to help you become the best possible version of yourself each day, every day.

Consider including these ten emotionally intelligent habits into your daily routines to help you better manage stressful situations, deal with difficult people, and embrace failure, change and uncertainty.

Develop a Practice of Self-Reflection

Adjust Your Monologue

Recognize Your Emotional Triggers

Embrace Empathic Communication

Take a Walk in Someone Else's Shoes

Observe How You Feel Often

Cultivate Your Curiosity About Others

Assess Your Assumptions

Risk Vulnerability

Eliminate Your "Ego-Speak"

Develop a Practice of Self-Reflection

From the moment we wake up in the morning until the moment we go to bed at night, our minds are whirring, churning, and in constant motion. They don't ever seem to shut off. We move around on auto-pilot, with our days overflowing with all sorts of "to-do's" that we can't seem to get to fast enough. Everything around us seems to command our attention and, sadly, the one thing that doesn't get as much attention as it should, is a mindful and open-minded reflection of ourselves.

Can you recall the last time you created a precious moment of solitude to reflect on how you're moving through this world? I venture to say that most of us would find it difficult to remember. If we don't become more deliberate about reflecting on own behavior and our interactions with others, we will continue to miss out on opportunities for personal growth.

The more aware you are of what's going on inside you, the better you're able to manage how it manifests externally—which, in turn, affects everything you do. Committing to a practice of solitude and self-reflection will allow you to challenge your own thoughts, possibly uncover breakthroughs, increase your self-awareness and ultimately allow you to live with more purpose and intention.

Below are some useful questions you can ask yourself as part of your practice of self-reflection:

1. Was I conscious of my self-talk today?

2. Did anything trigger me emotionally and, if so, how did I react to it?

3. Was I mindful of my choice of words in communicating with others?

4. Did I encounter any situations that raised questions or doubt in my mind?

5. Was I able to reframe them to Gateway questions?

6. Did I pay attention to how I felt today in general?

7. In my interactions with others, did I listen to understand?

8. Did I catch myself making any negative assumptions about people or situations?

9. Did I try to leave a positive emotional aftertaste for someone else?

Adjust Your Monologue

If you found yourself in the company of someone who complained incessantly and had a pessimistic view of life, how long would you voluntarily continue to associate with that person? Chances are, not very long. Interestingly enough, we sometimes have our own share of silent negativity and pessimism running through our minds and we allow these toxic thoughts (and resulting behaviors) to fester far longer than they ever should.

While our inner critic can be useful in pushing us to strive to be better, it often dominates the conversation negatively, adversely impacting our self-esteem, our attitudes and ultimately our treatment of others. The reality is that we hear our own voices the most and the loudest throughout our lives and it's vital that we create a deliberate practice of interrupting those runaway trains of negative thoughts that occasionally "choo-choo" their way through our minds.

One of the ways to do this is by becoming more vitally aware of how you talk to yourself. I'm pretty sure that the way you talk to yourself when you are happy is probably quite different than how you talk to yourself when you are angry, sad or confused. If you care about improving the quality of conversations you have with yourself, consider these three strategies:

1. **Speak to yourself as you would your best friend**
   If your best friend complained about an upcoming exam and lamented, "I am not good at this," your likely response might be, "Relax, you've prepared well. You got this." *Speak to yourself in the same way.*

2. **Create psychological distance from yourself** As professor of Psychology, Dr. Ethan Cross suggests, move from using first-person phrasing to third-person phrasing. For example, rather than asking yourself, "Why am I so stressed?" or, "How can I do better?" you can ask, "Why are *you* feeling so stressed?" Dr. Cross further explains that, "People who use the third-person 'you' begin to think of the task as a distant challenge rather than a direct threat.

3. **Use the words "I don't" more than you say "I can't"** Marketing professor Vanessa Patrick suggests, based on numerous studies, that people who use the phrase "I don't" to resist temptation fared better for longer than those who said "I can't." She believes that saying, "I can't" communicates limitation, whereas saying "I don't" is a powerful reminder that you're in charge of your thoughts and behavior.

Recognize Your Emotional Triggers

Each time you awake to the privilege of seeing another day, chances are, with that privilege will come with tests of your emotional endurance. Whether these tests are brought on by people you know, strangers or general life situations, how you deal with those emotional triggers, particularly in challenging moments, makes all the difference.

Through the example of my "chair-throwing incident," we saw firsthand the ramifications of poor emotional management. While it was perfectly fine for me to have felt all the emotions

I felt that day, how I chose to handle (or rather, *not* handle) my emotions transformed this singular experience into a regrettable life moment.

One of the ways we can better handle our triggers is by paying attention to the signals our bodies give us. For example, when you feel anger, you might tense up your muscles or grit your teeth—which is important information that can help you slow your mind down with some positive self-talk, while simultaneously taking a deep breath.

Once we can correctly identify the messages of our emotions, we can begin to manage them and respond to circumstances more effectively. In recognizing your triggers, developing a key word or phrase can become your saving grace in ensuring you appropriately *manage* being triggered. Maybe your go-to phrase is to quietly tell yourself to "calm down." Interesting enough, many people have told me that while saying "calm down" can be helpful if they say it quietly to themselves, they react negatively or defensively when they are told to calm down by someone else.

As you begin to pay closer attention to your own triggers, think of a situation at work or even at home where your effectiveness in accomplishing a task boils down to how well you manage your emotional triggers. Consider how you can influence your self-talk to serve rather than harm your opportunity to be successful.

Embrace Empathic Communication

Can you tell the difference when someone communicates with you empathically versus when they do not? After reading this book in its entirety, my hope is that you can certainly make this important distinction. You can probably tell because of how their communication style makes you feel. People who take the time to communicate with empathy meet our basic human desires to be treated with respect and to be understood.

If you reflect back on the example I shared in the first chapter which examined some of the myths surrounding EI, you'll recall that I made a point about the fact that empathy isn't about "being nice." In that example, you may recall that I spotlighted the compassion and empathy shown by an executive who reluctantly had to lay off fifteen percent of his staff.

In spite of this very difficult circumstance, he treated his departing staff with dignity and respect and communicated with them in ways that showed how much he understood their pain and heartbreak at losing their jobs.

If you have a desire to positively influence and impact others, communicating in ways that show how much you care about them is paramount to your success and effectiveness. We can all show more empathy in our own communication style in the simplest of ways. Here, I offer a few suggestions:

1. Notice how much you use the word "I" when speaking with others and eliminate it whenever possible. Using the first-person reference too often keeps your conversation very inwardly-turned and self-focused.

2. When listening to someone else, become aware about whether you're genuinely listening to understand them or just listening to respond.

3. Use empathic phrases often. For example, "I understand how that must make you feel..." or, "Can you help me understand..." or, "Let me see if I've heard you right..."

4. Keep an eye on your body language so you're not sending out the wrong signals. If, for instance, you're trying to make someone feel included or welcome, be sure not to have your arms crossed—or your back turned—at any time. Body language makes a difference.

Take a Walk in Someone Else's Shoes

It's fair to say that most of us have a basic human need to feel understood and valued, yet it often seems like we don't afford others the same opportunity. It goes without saying that the root of so much conflict and discord we experience in our personal lives, in the workplace and the world at large stems from our inability to walk in each other's shoes, to understand our differing perspectives, to display empathetic behavior.

Taking a walk in someone else's shoes can feel inconvenient, it can feel uncomfortable. Heck, it can even feel like a waste of time. If we peel back the layers to better understand why it can feel this way, my contention is that maybe it's in part because there is an unconscious reality we're escaping from. The reality that if we take a moment to understand someone else and walk in their shoes, we are forced to alter our thinking and our behavior in some way, which might not be something we're fully prepared to do.

As the saying goes, *"We fear what we don't understand,"* we also fear the unknown. Once we fill that gap (represented by the unknown) with understanding and knowledge, our fear of the "other" subsides. Put simply, knowledge itself often helps to dispel fear, confusion and anxiety.

Remember my client Karen who ultimately resolved a tumultuous work relationship with her co-worker by going out to lunch and making an effort to better understand her? As a result of each of them learning more about the other, their relationship improved dramatically and for the better.

What's key to remember is that stepping into someone else's shoes to understand their perspective doesn't mean you have to necessarily *agree* with them or even *approve of* them. The bottom line here, as Theodore Roosevelt reminds us, is that, "People don't care how much you know until they know how much you care."

Among the countless benefits you gain by exercising emotional intelligence and showing more empathy towards others, you gain influence and respect from the people with whom you interact.

As you dare to care about walking in someone else's shoes as often as possible, I challenge you to ask yourself an important, yet simple guiding question; a question that becomes even more relevant in tense or difficult times: "Am I making a genuine effort to understand them?"

Your answer should determine your resulting behavior.

Observe How You Feel Often

If I asked you to observe how you feel when you're happy, elated, blissful, or even content, I'm sure it would be an enjoyable and engaging task. It might even make you smile a little wider, reflecting on just how good you feel. If, on the other hand, I asked you to observe how you feel when you're dealing with difficult emotions like fear, anger, sadness or shame, this exercise would feel laborious and perhaps even threatening. In this instance, becoming more aware of your challenging emotions might create the unwanted effect of magnifying that feeling even further.

No matter how uncomfortable, however, it's still important to be aware of your emotions at any (and every) given moment, so that you remain in greater control of those emotions and more empowered to experience them productively.

As you observe how you're feeling, it's also vital to choose your words wisely and separate who you are from how you feel. It's in our moments of handling tough emotions that our self-talk seems to become most self-defeating. If for instance you experience shame, it's far more productive for you to say, "I *feel* shame" rather than to say, "I *am* ashamed." It can sound so trivial to interchange a word or two, but oftentimes—especially when it comes to our emotional intelligence—it's the small things that make the biggest difference.

As you get used to deliberately using the words "*I feel*" rather than, "*I am*," you train your mind to realize the impermanence of the emotion. It also helps you recognize that instead of taking up residence in your mind, the emotions you feel are simply passing through, like visiting houseguests. So, in essence, shame becomes something you *feel* and rather than something you *are*. Recognizing the distinction is imperative.

Let's test this out with a moderate emotion. As you begin to master this process, you can then try it out with stronger emotions like sadness or anger. For now, imagine you feel *annoyed* or *irritated* because of some critical feedback you received at work. Let's move directly into the moment:

1. *Identify how you feel*—"At this moment, I'm feeling annoyed and disappointed."

2. *Examine why you feel the way you do*—"I feel like I did everything I was told to do and I'm still being criticized for the outcome."

3. *Guide your self-talk productively*—"I choose to see this not as a personal attack, but as information that is critical to my growth."

4. *Let go of the need to control your emotion*—"It's perfectly normal for me to feel what I feel. It is to be experienced and not controlled."

Cultivate Your Curiosity About Others

Thanks to ever-evolving advances in modern technology, it's fair to say that we're living in a time in which we're more connected to each other than ever before, and yet in many ways, we couldn't be more disconnected from each other. This is an unfortunate paradox of our times: the "Social Media" phenomenon actually makes us far less social and far *more* isolated and separated from each other.

So, what do we do about it? Especially when we know that the happiest people are those with meaningful and sustained connections in their lives? Well, one of the ways we get back to creating deeper and more meaningful connections is by showing a genuine interest and curiosity in others. Even the busiest among us can still make time for this.

Think about how good you feel when someone pays attention to you and shows a genuine interest in what you have to say.

Doesn't it satisfy a basic need to be seen and heard? I think a little reciprocity is fair game, wouldn't you agree? Having a healthy curiosity for others doesn't only make you more emotionally intelligent, it also makes you an interesting, compassionate, and responsible human being.

Cultivating a curiosity about other cultures, other cuisines and places around the world makes your life richer and more interesting. This is one of the biggest reasons that countless people around the globe fell in love with the late celebrity chef and culinary adventurer Anthony Bourdain.

With his critically acclaimed travel TV show, he successfully aroused a genuine curiosity in his viewers through his magnificent portrayals of people, culture, and cuisine far different from our own.

Remember that when others see you take a genuine interest in them, they open up more and that helps you build trust and influence.

Assess Your Assumptions

It's almost instinctual for us to make assumptions about other people and about our surroundings. When we're faced with unknowns or incomplete information, our natural tendency is to fill in those knowledge gaps with our own assumptions.

It would be unrealistic or disingenuous of me to tell you to stop making assumptions altogether, because sometimes, it's in our best interests to make assumptions. We just want to be mindful to make *healthy*, non-judgmental assumptions that serve us rather than sabotage our efforts, both personally and professionally.

If you recall my experience as a Lyft driver, which I shared at the outset of this book, when I was confronted by a passenger who was less than polite, I allowed my ego to jump into the front seat of my mind and I began to make a lot of assumptions about her which fueled my rage and negative self-talk.

Whenever you're confronted with a situation that feels unknown or unfamiliar, stop for a moment and pay deliberate attention to whether you're making any assumptions. If you are, assess whether you've put a positive or negative spin on them. Also ask yourself if there is any other way of viewing what lies before you. Be purposeful in your thinking and slow in your tendency to jump to inaccurate assumptions.

Risk Vulnerability

Every day we wake up and leave our houses to live our lives. The truth of the matter is that there is a risk that it might be our last day on earth—even our final moment of living—yet we still go out and carry on with our day without harping on what we might lose in the process. And yet when it comes to risking vulnerability, we tend to focus most heavily on what we stand to lose if things don't quite go our way—and it is this thought pattern and resulting behavior that prevents us from being bold in our living.

While it true, as Dr. Brené Brown writes, that "vulnerability is uncertainty, risk, and emotional exposure," she also adds that "it is our most accurate measure of courage." The brilliant Dr. Brown could not be more correct.

Most of us think about vulnerability as anything that exposes us to emotions we'd much rather escape than experience, and yet the idea of opening ourselves up to potential feelings of pain, fear, sadness or shame is one of the most courageous things we can do for ourselves.

The more you practice opening yourself up to being vulnerable, the easier it will begin to actually *feel*. When you think about your fears (as we all do), like a fear of rejection or a fear of being judged, ask yourself, *what is the worst that can happen if my fear comes true?* As you think more about this, you may find that the outcome is not as bad as you expect, not even in the worst-case scenario.

In those moments of vulnerability, remember that as human beings, we are hard-wired to feel shame, which is actually normal. The key is not to focus on the potential of feeling ashamed but rather on what you stand to gain for exercising your vulnerability muscles.

Eliminate Your Ego-Speak

Despite a lot of talk about how toxic and destructive our egos can become, there are some ways our egos benefit us. It's what prevents us from being pushed around or bullied or even roped into believing everything negative someone has to say about us. Aside from the few instances where it can serve us, our egos play a combative role against our quest to grow our EI, whether it's by convincing us that we are superior to others or, conversely, making us feel inferior.

We tend to engage in *ego-speak* most often when we're feeling vulnerable and don't want to admit that either we're wrong, or we don't feel good enough, or we don't want to get introspective and reflect on our behavior and our flaws or we don't want to see things from someone else's perspective.

When we allow our egos to speak for us, when we allow our insecurities to drive our thinking and our behavior, it leaves no room for empathy, compassion, understanding, and self-correction—and these things stand at the heart of the true definition of emotional intelligence.

Here are six examples of our ego speaking louder than our best judgment:

1. You feel jealous when other people do well;

2. You talk about yourself without showing much interest in hearing from others;

3. You have a desire to always win and be right;

4. If you're in a heated debate, you can't back down until you've won the argument, and,

5. You set yourself impossible goals and berate yourself when you don't achieve these goals.

As you endeavor to keep your ego out of the driver's seat, know that it's going to take a lot of conscious practice and deliberate effort to listen out for your ego and put it in its rightful place—but doing so is imperative if you want to walk through life with clarity, humility and an open mind.

Your journey to greater emotional intelligence does indeed begin with one step, followed by one more, and then yet another. Just like that beautiful butterfly to which Dr. Angelou referred in the opening quote of this chapter, your journey ahead may not be easy and it will take work to make these emotionally intelligent habits a seamless part of your daily life. But as you do, watch the transformative difference it will make in your life and the lives of those you impact.

With hard work, clarity of thinking, and constant effort, you can, indeed, *be* the butterfly. You can, indeed, be the Simone Biles and the Usain Bolt.

Let the journey begin!

CONCLUSION
My Final, Five-Word Challenge

"People will forget what you said, people will forget what you did, but people will never forget how you made them feel."
— Dr. Maya Angelou

Friday, March 14th, 2003.
A day I will never forget.

I STILL REMEMBER THE TENSION and sadness in my older brother Edwin's voice as he spoke to me from his home in Ghana.

Behind his brave attempt to sound steady and calm, the whispered words he spoke crashed through all of his confidence. They were words I never wanted to hear. Never hoped to hear. Never imagined I'd *ever* hear.

"Sylvia, you and Kofi should try to get on the next flight home. Daddy is in the hospital and he's really trying to hold on."

I knew it instinctively: My father, my brave protector, my brilliant motivator, was about to leave me. My superhero was about to slip away. I could already feel the yawning gap of grief open up before me. I prayed for him to hold on just a little longer; to stay strong for just a moment longer, until I could get there to say my final goodbye.

When my twin brother and I arrived in Accra two days later, we went straight to the hospital to see him. He had been hanging on, waiting for us, and the moment we walked into his room, his eyes lit up with an unforgettable radiance.

In the faintest trace of his signature deep voice, he mustered just enough energy to whisper, "I'm soooo happy to see you." The final sparkle in his eyes told me how much he meant those words.

It had been two years since Kofi and I last saw him and those simple yet cherished words would be his last, because his doctor inserted a tube into his trachea shortly thereafter.

A week to the day after we arrived by his side, my Daddy, my hero, and the man who enriched and even saved the lives of so many (including my own), breathed his last breath.

He slipped away.

At his funeral, on a brilliant Thursday afternoon in early April, I was blown away by just how many people came to say their last goodbyes to this incredibly humble and unassuming man who clearly left an indelible mark on their hearts and minds. They came from all parts of the country, from all corners of the earth, from all walks of life, and it was indeed a sight to behold.

Daddy was an absolute class act, and beyond everything he accomplished personally and professionally in his fifty-six years on earth, all the heartwarmingly touching tributes pointed directly to the power and the lasting, positive effect he had on others.

In the twenty-five years he was present in my life, my father never uttered the words "emotional intelligence" (the term hadn't yet become mainstream). He never *had* to, because he lived it wholeheartedly each and every day.

Before it even became a buzzword, before it became a popular practice, before it even became an abstract concept, *my father had singlehandedly defined the meaning of Emotional Intelligence.*

He had a remarkable ability to manage his emotions, even in the toughest of times, and he jumped at every opportunity to make others feel valued, validated and heard. Daddy lived his emotional intelligence out loud.

If you are reading these words right now, you have one thing my father no longer has. You have the promise of the present. You have life left in you, you have air to breathe, you have potential to realize and a future that promises to unfold before you. You, my readers, you have the opportunity to live your emotional intelligence out loud. And now, you must use this opportunity to become the best possible version of yourself every single day.

In the beginning of this book, we set out to answer three critical questions:

- How can I use my emotions to work for me and not against me?
- Why should I care about how others feel?
- What does it take to have more satisfying and rewarding relationships?

Through absorbing the life lessons within this book, as well as anything you may already know about emotional intelligence, I hope you continue to ask yourself these questions to ensure you're doing what it takes to manage your emotions and their impact on others. This will ensure you pave the way for those deep and meaningful connections that are so necessary for the soul.

Let your emotions work for you: by committing to a practice of frequent self-reflection; by recognizing your "lizards" and emotional triggers, so that you remain empowered when they come slithering into your day; and by keeping a close eye on your self-talk to ensure that in those testy and challenging moments you don't create destructive thoughts that lead to self-defeating actions.

If you're like me, you want to feel like you matter, like your presence makes some sort of difference. If that is the case, caring about your impact on others is not just an option: *It is a mandate.*

Harness your EI skills to help you. Cultivate a curiosity about others. Take a walk in someone else's shoes as often as possible. Risk being vulnerable. These are the ways you build connection, trust and influence. These are the ways you not only seek—but *find*—emotional intelligence.

No truer words have been spoken than the words of Dr. Maya Angelou's that appear at the beginning of this section, reminding us that above and beyond anything we do or achieve in our time on this earth, the way we treat others will have the most lasting and far-reaching impact.

It has been a pleasure, a joy, a distinct and somber honor, having you accompany me on this journey towards emotional intelligence, and it is my hope—my prayer—that you will continue to nourish and nurture your emotional intelligence. No one else can do it except you.

But mine is far more than a passive prayer. Mine is far more than an ardent hope. My wish for you to continue walking this path towards EI is far more than a *wish*. It is a challenge. It is a plea.

It is a directive that stems straight from my heart and consists of five, simple words; words that my father lived to the fullest every, single, solitary day of his precious life. Remember them always:

I dare you to care.

ACKNOWLEDGMENTS

THERE IS AN AFRICAN PROVERB that says, "If you want to go fast, go alone. If you want to go far, go together."

Bringing *I Dare You to Care* to life could not have been possible without the help and support of a large group of folks. While I know that a simple acknowledgment and name mention doesn't begin to convey the depth of my gratitude for your undying encouragement, I hope you already know just how much your support has meant to me.

I begin with my biggest cheerleader, my husband, Alfonso. Thank you for serving up the occasional glass of my favorite Cabernet Sauvignon to celebrate the small wins along the way. Your loving loyalty sustains me.

Kristin Clark Taylor, the lessons I absorbed from you as you masterfully edited my work allowed my voice to shine through in a way it otherwise wouldn't. You gave me my writing wings, pushing me to leap beyond what I thought possible and I can't thank you enough for your persistence and dedication.

A special thank-you to Candace Ford, Chyann Oliver, Kisa Mfalila, Patricia Okolo, and cousin Sophie Baffour for all those thought-provoking conversations about emotional intelligence that opened my mind to new ways of thinking.

Diana Watson, a special thank-you for being my original writing buddy all the way in Taiwan. All those Skype calls and story writing sessions we had kickstarted this journey for me.

To those who contributed to the interview or research-gathering phase, I am deeply grateful for your precious time and invaluable insight. Thank you, Ashley Lanton, Courtney Wright, Brandon Frazier, Joren Lindholm, Aisha Evans, U'mau Otuokon, Fredanna McGough, Marie Hunt, Melonie McCall, Fred Hall, Shelja Purohit, Jen Renteria, Meme Fehmers, Tamae Takahashi, and Emily Kenlaw.

A special mention to my dear friend and Public Relations guru, Beverly Hunt, for your priceless wisdom and tireless dedication.

My other supporters and cheerleaders, you're the best. Because I have a very large family, I will simply say, *Thank you, fam*. You know who you are. Thank you also to dear friends Leonard Manning, Wendy Marie Thomas, Cristina Flores, Christie Cook, Ira Koretsky, Joanna Kosmides Edwards, and Paul Nicholas, for your faithful friendship.

Together, we have gone far and your selfless contributions continue to leave a sweet emotional aftertaste in my heart and mind forever!

ABOUT THE AUTHOR

SYLVIA BAFFOUR IS A PROFESSIONAL speaker, trainer, and executive coach ranked among HubSpot's Top Fifteen Female Motivational Speakers. She is the founder and president of Baffour International LLC, an organization committed to improving how individuals and companies leap beyond their barriers to achieve peak performance.

Her roots began more than four decades ago in her native country of Ghana, and since the tender age of one and a half, her life's journey has taken her through several countries across the globe.

Sylvia is one of the most sought-after speakers and trainers in the fields of personal empowerment and professional development and she is a highly respected thought leader in Emotional Intelligence.

For more information on her speaking
and coaching services, please visit:
www.sylviaspeaks.com
info@sylviaspeaks.com